T0322151

HARD STUFF, EASY LIFE

HARD STUFF, EASY LIFE

7 Mindset Principles for Success,
Strength and Happiness

JAY ALDERTON

MICHAEL JOSEPH
PENGUIN
Est. 1936

PENGUIN MICHAEL JOSEPH

UK | USA | Canada | Ireland | Australia
India | New Zealand | South Africa

Penguin Michael Joseph is part of the Penguin Random House
group of companies whose addresses can be found at
global.penguinrandomhouse.com

First published by Penguin Michael Joseph, 2024

001

Copyright © Jay Alderton, 2024

Quotes: p. 5 Permission granted by The Viktor Frankl Institute; p. 8
Permission granted by Dr Linda Humphreys; p. 17 Permission granted by
Zig Ziglar; p. 41 Permission granted by Robert Brault; p. 159 Permission
granted by Karen Blixen Group. Images: p. 87: © Feodora Rosca/Alamy
Stock Vector; p. 122 © iStock.com/budi priyanto; p. 124 Permission granted
by simplypsychology.org: https://www.simplypsychology.org/cognitive-
distortions-in-cbt.html; p. 125 © iStock.com/cnythzl; p. 144 iStock.com/
PICTEORICO; p. 164 © iStock.com/Heather Stokes; p. 205 © iStock.com/
DragonTiger

The moral right of the author has been asserted

Set in TT Norms Pro

Typeset by Couper Street Type Co.

Printed in Great Britain by Clays Ltd, Elcograf S.p.A.

The authorized representative in the EEA is Penguin Random House Ireland,
Morrison Chambers, 32 Nassau Street, Dublin D02 YH68

A CIP catalogue record for this book is available from the British Library

HARDBACK ISBN: 978-0-241-68267-8

TRADE PAPERBACK ISBN: 978-1-405-96370-1

This book is dedicated to my family, friends and failures.

To my wife, Anna; daughter, Elyza; and son, Archer
– you bring light and joy into my world. I'm so
thankful to have you by my side every day.

To my friends Dr Mike, Shaa, Dan, Phil and Jason. You are
among the most influential people in my life. Thanks to your
success, support and friendship, you inspire me to be better.

To my failures. I'm grateful for each and every one
of you. Without failing, I wouldn't learn, grow and
improve. Please keep visiting me so I can learn life's
hard lessons on the path to an easier life.

The Hard Stuff, Easy Life Principles

Principle 1: Happiness is an Inside Job

You might have heard the song 'Don't Worry Be Happy'. Well . . . this principle goes one step further. Happiness is not something that just comes to you or a destination that you arrive at; it's a feeling you can choose to have, no matter what's happening around you.

Principle 2: Make Peace With Your Past

We all have things in our past that we're not proud of, but dwelling on past mistakes only robs you of your current joy and future success. I've realized this from my mistakes in business and relationships, too. Holding on to a negative past makes focusing on a positive future impossible.

Principle 3: Love Yourself

Self-love isn't about narcissism or selfishness; it's about acknowledging your worth and value as a human being. Your opinion of yourself should not be entirely reliant on external validation. I learned from my own experiences that loving yourself comes first, and it helps you love others better.

Principle 4: No One Cares

One of the biggest barriers that holds us back from pursuing goals and overcoming challenges is the fear of judgement or ridicule. We imagine all eyes are focused on us, harshly evaluating our every move. This illusion of being under society's merciless microscope fuels self-doubt and anxiety. How often do you pay close attention to strangers around you? Probably almost never. Their actions or choices, even embarrassments, barely register in your consciousness. The same is true in reverse.

Principle 5: Don't Allow Feelings to Affect Your Future

Feelings come and go, but your actions can affect you for a long time. It's essential to act based on what you want to achieve, not just how you feel at the moment. In my life, there have been many days when I didn't want to wake up early and do what needed to be done, but doing it anyway helped me deal with future challenges and made them easier to deal with, too.

Principle 6: Be Present

With limitless distractions at the touch of a button in our pockets, it's easy to miss out on the here and now. Paying full attention to the current moment makes life better and more enjoyable. Just like when our phones are playing up and we need to turn them off to work well again, sometimes, we need to switch off our phones and focus on what's in front of us to feel better.

Principle 7: Hard Stuff, Easy Life; Easy Stuff, Hard Life

This principle is the cornerstone of the book. I've learned that doing the hard stuff, whether gruelling physical tasks, challenging emotional work or hard strategic thinking, makes the rest of life fall into place more smoothly. On the other hand, always choosing the easy stuff can make your life more complicated and challenging.

Introduction

The Problem Is in Your Head

L ife is full of challenges and problems. It's very easy to pinpoint multiple things responsible for our successes and failures: economic downturns, demanding bosses and social media. If you can name it, we've probably blamed it!

It can sometimes feel that the world is conspiring against us, and we can do nothing but try our best to avoid the hard stuff life throws at us. But what if I told you that's all an illusion?

The truth is, what's inside our head daily, our thoughts, our emotions and our beliefs, dictate how we absorb and respond to all these external events.

It's not that these outside influences don't exist or aren't challenging . . . but they don't have to define us or our capacity for happiness and success.

Our mind is like a lens through which we see the world; if it's clouded with negativity, we see challenges as threats rather than what we really should see them as, and that's opportunities for growth.

My mission with this book is to share a series of principles that help you understand that many of life's difficulties start with a simple shift inside your head. You are not just some passive spectator sitting on the sidelines of success but an active participant in your own life, and it's about time you took control of the narrative.

Something we often fall into in life is seeing ourselves as passive recipients of difficulties. We believe life's challenges are happening to us rather than being opportunities for growth. In this book, through each principle, I will show you that you hold the power to change your perspective on challenges and reshape your life in a positive way.

It's your mental outlook that dictates your physical actions, and it's your physical actions that dictate your life. This is why the journey to a successful, strong and happy life starts not in the gym or your job but in your thoughts.

The Mindset Shift: From Victim to Victor

My way of thinking wasn't always like this. As a teenager, I was unfocused, distracted and had zero direction. Because of this, I was drinking heavily, getting into trouble, and I realized after failing college that there were only two paths for me to take. Continue distracting myself with pleasure and end up in prison or make a drastic shift in my life and join the army.

It was not an easy decision, but in October 2003 I boarded a train, sick with worry and nerves, to start day one of basic training.

During those seven years of British Army service, I was compelled to confront my weaknesses and limitations. There was no room for excuses, only room for growth. And so, from a reluctant, aimless teenager, I slowly morphed into a disciplined, focused individual.

'When a person can't find a deep sense of meaning, they distract themselves with pleasure'

– Viktor E. Frankl

The army gave me five tools I have continued to carry through my life:

Discipline: army life is highly structured, with rules dictating everything you do from when you wake up to when you go to sleep. This regimented environment instilled a strong sense of discipline in me and got me to understand the word's true meaning. Doing things regardless of how you feel, because life becomes easier when you do the hard stuff.

Teamwork and Camaraderie: the army involves working closely with others, often in challenging and stressful conditions. This instilled a deep sense of teamwork and the ability to cooperate with people from diverse backgrounds and perspectives. I didn't know it at the time, but this taught me social skills, which are fundamental when it comes to living a healthier and happier life.

Leadership Skills: as a soldier, I was given responsibilities at a young age that required me to lead others. This taught me to make quick decisions, often under pressure, and to take initiative and lead by example. It wasn't until I looked back at this that I realized just how important this has been for my growth as a person.

Mental and Physical Toughness: the rigorous training and stressful situations I encountered in the army taught me resilience and fortitude. Physical fitness (the ability to execute daily activities with optimal performance, endurance and strength) improves with practice, and mental toughness (learning how to cope with stress, fear and fatigue) improves with practice, too.

Sense of Purpose and Service: serving in the army instilled a strong sense of duty and purpose in me, offering me an opportunity to be part of something bigger than myself. This gave me a valuable perspective, taught me the power of community and shared responsibility and has held me accountable for getting things done.

The Self-Fulfilling Prophecy

One of the most potent psychological insights that can transform your life is the understanding that your perception moulds your reality. Experts in psychology and neuroscience have always been fascinated by how we understand the world around us.

Our perception isn't just about receiving information like a computer taking in data, it's an active process in which we give meaning to what we see, hear and feel. How we interpret these experiences influences our actions, how we respond to situations and even how we view ourselves.

One theory that explains this is the concept of the self-fulfilling prophecy.

Sociologist Robert Merton initially proposed this theory, and he put forward that our beliefs about a situation or person could influence our behaviour towards that situation or person, causing us to act in a way that causes those beliefs to come true.

Basically, if you think you're going to fail, you're less likely to put in the effort needed to succeed. It's your lack of action that, in turn, causes the very failure you were dreading, which then reinforces your original perception.

The Power of Perception

One story that I love to hear about the power of perception is that of Roger Bannister. He was the first man to break the four-minute mile, but before he did experts believed it was impossible

'Perception moulds, shapes and influences our experience of our personal reality'

– Dr Linda Humphreys

and some said even deadly. It was this perception that held many athletes back from attempting it. They had mentally imposed a barrier on their performance.

However, Bannister refused to accept this perception and he pushed himself beyond this imaginary limit. When he broke the four-minute barrier in 1954, something incredible happened. More runners started breaking it, too. The reality is that the physical attributes of the athletes hadn't changed; it was the perception of what was possible.

Back in 2019 I was deep into my training for a Guinness World Record feat that no one had dared attempt before – box jumping the height of Mount Everest in under twenty-four hours. This challenge boiled down to jumping on to a two-foot box 14,516 times, averaging between thirteen and fifteen jumps per minute.

When I finally started the event, a flood of perceptions came into my mind . . .

No one's done this because it's humanly impossible!

You've only trained up to eight hours. How will your body withstand another sixteen?

You'll probably get rhabdomyolysis, breaking down muscle to the point of kidney damage or death!

I tuned out the naysaying and pressed on. At the eight-hour mark, everything was still on track. But shortly after disaster struck – a pulled calf muscle and quadriceps cramps slowed me down dramatically. Panic started setting in.

What if they're right? What if my body can't take sixteen more agonizing hours of this torture?

I needed to shift my thinking fast or I'd never make it. A new mental tactic emerged. *Don't focus on the full twenty-four hours. Instead, concentrate only on completing the next hour.*

I had calculated needing to complete the jumps in twenty-two rather than twenty-four hours in order to have a buffer. This required 660 jumps per hour instead of 605. I'd need to allow short recovery breaks each hour without sacrificing pace.

In the ninth hour, with my calf screaming and lactic acid searing through my quads, old doubts resurfaced. *How can I possibly keep this up?*

Rather than fixating on the next fifteen hours, I zoomed my focus to simply finishing the next twenty-five minutes strong. Smaller milestones brought my mind to the present moment. All my energy was focused just on completing each milestone.

In those painful final minutes when my body begged to quit, my mind remained unbroken, anchored in the current hour's completion. And at long last, after what turned out to be 14,550 jumps and twenty-two hours of blood, sweat and tears – victory!

On 30 November 2019, I officially became the first and the fastest person to box jump Mount Everest, forever a Guinness World Record holder. And it never would have happened without shifting my thinking to an hour-by-hour battle plan.

This idea is simple but transformative: change your perception, change your life. Perception sets the boundaries of what you believe is achievable. By altering those boundaries, even just a little, you open doors to possibilities that were inconceivable under your previous mindset. Whether running a business, improving your health or enhancing your relationships, mastering the power of perception could be your first step towards a life filled with success, strength and happiness.

As we delve deeper into the seven mindset principles in this book, remember that these are not just rules to follow but

The problem and the solution
are both in your head.

transformative shifts in perception that can create a new reality for you. The problem and the solution are both in your head.

The Truth About Discipline

An Introduction to True Discipline

When we talk about discipline, various images might spring to mind. The King's Guards at Buckingham Palace standing tall and not allowing anything to distract them from doing their job, the musician who effortlessly plays the piano in ways you've never heard before or the athlete who's up before sunrise to complete a gruelling workout before the day has even started.

While these examples show some aspects of discipline, they also spread misunderstandings about it. By believing these myths, we accidentally make it harder for ourselves, making discipline seem like something only a few special people have. Before discussing *what* discipline is, it's essential to clear up these misunderstandings and explain what discipline *is NOT*.

Discipline Helps You Win

First, let's debunk the myth that discipline means being stiff and having no freedom. People think if you're disciplined, you stick to a strict set of rules and never change them. This is not true. Strong self-discipline doesn't limit your life; it gives you structure that helps you improve it. Discipline is like knowing the rules of a game; once you understand them, you can play freely and even win.

Change your perception, change your life.

Discipline Is a Life Skill

Another myth is that you're either born with or without discipline. Some people believe that discipline is like height or eye colour in that it's a fixed attribute you can't change. If I've shown anything in this chapter, you can go from a directionless, unfocused school kid following all the wrong paths and completely change into a different person over time. Discipline is a skill, and it's something that can be cultivated through practice and mindful application.

Discipline Gives You Control

Yet another harmful belief is that discipline means punishing yourself and not allowing yourself to enjoy things. Some people think being disciplined means constantly avoiding fun and making life hard for yourself. Discipline isn't about punishing yourself; it's about gaining, or regaining, control over your actions. It helps you make choices that move you closer to your goals, even when they are hard.

Discipline Makes You Wiser

And the final myth to put to bed is that discipline means you never make mistakes or fail. Thinking this is true sets a standard that's way too high, making achieving self-discipline seem out of reach. The truth is everyone fails sometimes. (I think I've failed more times than I've succeeded.)

What truly makes a disciplined person is what they do when they make that mistake or even fail. They learn from their mistakes or failures and then use them to get back on the right path, having learned the lesson from the mistake or failure.

As we go on, let's forget these false ideas and make space for a better, more helpful understanding of discipline. True discipline isn't about being stiff, being born with it, punishing yourself or never failing. It's about creating good habits and ways of thinking that help you succeed in the long run. It's about becoming someone who can handle life's ups and downs well. It's something that anyone can learn.

True Discipline: Doing It Even When You Don't Want To

To me, discipline means doing what needs to be done, especially when you don't want to. It's the backbone of every significant achievement of mine and the principles underpinning this book.

Doing the Hard Stuff Makes Life Easy

It might sound paradoxical but it's true. Throughout my life, I've encountered numerous challenges – gruelling physical tasks and emotionally draining experiences. Every time I embraced these difficulties instead of avoiding them, I came out stronger, more resilient and better prepared for future challenges. The rest of my life seemed to fall into place more smoothly. Simply put, doing the hard stuff turned out to be an investment in a more manageable, fulfilling future.

Why Does Discipline Matter?

So why does discipline matter in all these areas? Because it's universally applicable. Discipline is not specific to a job or a situation; it's a life skill. No matter the context, the practice of discipline leads to outcomes that are generally beneficial for the individual and whatever group they are part of. Whether it's in relationships, work or personal development, discipline sets the stage for meeting and exceeding expectations.

Discipline isn't just about doing things right; it's about doing the right things mainly when it's hard to do so. Once you understand and integrate discipline into your daily life, you'll find that the most challenging paths often lead to the most rewarding destinations.

The Seven Mindset Principles

In the following chapters, I will dive deep into my seven mindset principles for success, strength and happiness, weaving in a story or two to get you thinking outside the box.

Although these stories are fictional, they are far from theoretical; the principles they convey have been rigorously field-tested through my life experiences, from the discipline instilled in me during my time in the British Army to the business and athletic challenges I've faced and conquered. These principles will be broken down in an easy-to-understand manner, illustrated with short stories that give them a framework which will help you write your own story. If anything, my role is to do my best to help you rise to the challenge.

The seven mindset principles have not just been plucked out of thin air but I have lived and breathed them. And the good news? They can be applied to your life, too. As we go through each principle, you'll learn how to implement them in your journey towards success, strength and happiness, making it fully your own.

'Difficult roads often lead to beautiful destinations'

\- Zig Ziglar

It's Not About Me, It's About You

I want to clarify that this book is not a memoir or a biography about me. While I've used a couple of personal stories about myself to highlight fundamental principles and the frameworks for understanding them, my greatest ambition is to give you actionable steps to help you create a healthier, happier and stronger life. It's not about reminiscing over my achievements and successes; far from it, it's about transferring the lessons I've learned from those experiences into guidelines you can apply to your own life.

Instead of just stating principles, I'm using simple short stories to help you grasp each one better. When we connect with story characters, our brain releases a feel-good hormone called oxytocin. This hormone helps us feel close to the people in the story and understand the message behind them that they want us to learn.

A confession from me is that I often find myself getting emotional when watching certain Disney movies with my kids. The characters' challenges in these films make me think about my life. For example, a specific scene in the movie *Coco* makes me ponder the inevitability of growing older and eventually having to say goodbye to my children. It's a reminder for me to make the most of the time I have with them.

Why this book?

So why did I write this book? Simply put, I've seen first-hand how transformative it can be to approach life with the right mindset. From my teen years, where I had no sense of direction and lived for the moment, to joining the British Army at seventeen and learning about discipline, resilience and the importance of a growth mindset, my transformation has been profound. But I'm just one example. Every one of us has the capacity for change, growth and tremendous achievement if only we adjust our approach to the stuff life throws at us.

My drive for writing this book lies in a mission that I've been focused on for many years now: leaving people better than when they found me. You might be stuck in a rut at your job, or perhaps you're struggling with some confidence issues; it might be that you're looking to give yourself a complete life overhaul or simply a few upgrades. No matter your situation, I genuinely believe that my seven mindset principles will serve as a stepping stone on your path to a healthier, happier and stronger life.

By the end of this book, I aim for you to see life through a different lens. I want you to understand that happiness is a state of mind you can choose regardless of circumstances. I want to help you make peace with your past and be excited for a fresh new start with unlimited possibilities. I aim to inspire you to love yourself more, to stop caring so much about what others think of you, and live your life as much in the present as possible. Above everything, I aim to get you to embrace the idea that doing the hard stuff now makes life easier down the road.

By sharing these principles with my short stories and personal experiences, my mission is to equip you for your own personal transformation physically, mentally and emotionally because at the end of the day it's not about what I've done or where I've been; it's about where you're going and how you're going to get there.

I want this book to be your guide, personal mentor and your energy and inspiration for an exciting journey ahead. I want this book to be your roadmap to navigate the challenges and enjoy the rewards of choosing a life filled with hard stuff that leads to an easy life.

Your Personal Invitation to Change

I want to warmly invite you to embrace change. If you've picked up this book, chances are that you're looking for ways to improve your life, tackle life's challenges more effectively or find a deeper sense of happiness and fulfilment. Whatever your motivation or drive, I want to assure you that the answers you seek are within your grasp and, more importantly, within you.

As you go through the chapters, remember that this book isn't just a manual or guide; it's a personal invitation from me. It's an offer for you to open your mind up to new ways of thinking, challenge your current beliefs and attitudes and try to see the world and yourself in a new light – a light that helps you 'see' paths you may never have considered walking.

Five Quick Tips for Approaching This Book

Stay Open-Minded

Be open to ideas or principles that might seem strange. Try not to dismiss them; instead, try to understand the reason behind them and why I've included them in this book. Doing so might help you discover a valuable idea or perspective you've never considered before.

*Doing the hard stuff now makes
life easier down the road.*

Keep Track

Use your brain for thinking, not for remembering. Keep a note-pad or your phone handy to write down any ideas or feelings that resonate with you and then revisit them as you apply the principles to your life. I've also left extra space after each chapter specifically for that purpose, as well as at the back of the book, so write away. This book should not be left untouched. It should be the witness to your change and progress.

Break the Rules

A short story accompanies each principle to illustrate its core idea. After reading them, try to apply the principle to a small aspect of your life and make a note of the results. Feel free to play around and mix and match, too. You're not a slave to the order in which the principles are laid out. Following them step by step is an option, choosing one principle and sticking to it for a chosen period of time another. There is no going wrong here.

Absorb and Apply

Don't just skim through the pages; at the end of each principle will be some tasks. Absorb the content, reflect on it and challenge yourself to complete one of the action steps on the day you read the chapter.

Be Patient

Change isn't something that happens overnight. It's an endless journey that requires time, effort and persistence. Like Aesop's

Slow and steady always wins the race.

fable of the tortoise and the hare, slow and steady always wins the race.

The title of this introduction, 'The Problem Is In Your Head', isn't meant to be taken lightly. It aims to underscore the power of your mind and perception in shaping your reality. It's easy to think that life just happens *to us* and that we're along for the ride, but when we finally start to change the way we think and adjust the lens through which we see the world, we don't just change our perception of it – we change our whole reality.

The 'problem' is in your head but remember – so is the *solution*. In your mind lies incredible power. The power to adapt, the power to overcome and the power to create the life you've always wanted. It's all about viewing challenges not as obstacles but as opportunities. It's about understanding that discipline is not a form of punishment but a pathway to freedom.

These seven principles have entirely changed my life in ways I could have never imagined. From a directionless teen to my transformative years in the British Army and my career shifts and accomplishments over the years, these principles have been the foundations on which I have built my experiences.

Let's embark on this journey together. As you turn the page, keep your mind open to the boundless possibilities and remember that the power to change your life rests only with you and your mind.

Principle 1

Happiness is an Inside Job

The Bird and the Tree

A single withered tree stood in a vast, sun-baked desert where the endless golden sands spread out under the sky. The tree had faced many arduous years in this harsh environment. Its branches were all twisted up, and its bark was rough and dried. The tree had seen better times and often moaned about living in such an empty place.

Near the tree was a small oasis, a rare gem in the desert. Here, a tiny bird with feathers as colourful as the oasis made its home. Despite the desert's toughness, the bird was always flying happily, its sweet songs filling the air.

The bird would sing every morning as the sun rose, shining its intense rays over the land. Its tunes were like calm winds, relieving the hot earth. The tree, though, didn't find any comfort in them. It grumbled about the never-ending sun, the lack of water and being so alone.

'Why do you sing, little bird?' the tree asked one day, its voice as dry as the desert sands. 'Look around; it's just heat and nothingness. Why be happy?'

The bird sat on one of the tree's brittle branches, thinking. 'I sing because I choose to see the good in every day,' it answered brightly. 'Yes, the desert is tough, but it's also my home. It has a stark beauty, a strength that I love. Happiness, dear tree, isn't about where you are but how you see your world.'

The tree didn't believe this. How could anyone find joy in such a bleak place? Yet each day the bird returned with its songs, its spirit not dimmed by the rough surroundings. Slowly, the tree started to wonder. What if it tried to see the world like the bird did? The tree began to notice things it could be thankful for. It saw how its branches gave shade to tired travellers. It admired the rare desert flowers that grew at its base. The tree even started feeling proud of its deep roots, which had kept it standing through many storms.

As days went by, something unique happened. The tree found itself complaining less. The sun seemed less hot, the winds less harsh. The tree felt peaceful, happy even, for the first time in years.

One morning, as the bird sang its dawn song, the tree realized it was no longer just a withered tree in a lonely desert. It was part of something bigger, a sign of survival and strength. And, with that thought, the tree began to bloom, small delicate flowers appearing on its bare branches.

Once a place of sorrow, the desert had become a source of beauty and strength. The tree had learned that happiness wasn't about the outside world but an inner choice to make every day, no matter what was happening around it. From then on, the bird's songs weren't the only happiness in the desert. The once withered tree stood as a beacon of hope, symbolizing the joy that can come from within.

The Happiness Illusion

Many people mistakenly equate happiness with intense euphoria and excitement. However, this couldn't be further from the truth. I vividly recall my wedding day in 2007 – undeniably one of the happiest days of my life. Yet, amid this joy, I also remember feeling utterly exhausted and being swept up in a whirlwind of emotions. Happiness isn't just about these moments of intense feelings.

Excitement and euphoria often stem from a surge of neurotransmitters like dopamine and endorphins, creating a temporary high that's sometimes confused with happiness. But this high is fleeting. Our bodies can't sustain such heightened states for long. In contrast, happiness – a state of well-being – isn't reliant on these intense neurochemical responses.

True happiness is far more complex and multifaceted. It resembles a garden cultivated with peace, satisfaction and a sense of purpose. It's discovered in the quieter moments of contentment and joy, meaningful relationships and personal growth. Recognizing the difference has altered my approach to life. I've moved away from the relentless pursuit of fleeting highs, focusing instead on the more lasting aspects of well-being.

It's important not to dismiss the value of excitement and pleasure. These experiences can enrich our lives, adding colour and vitality. But mistaking them for true happiness can lead us to constantly pursue short-lived highs. In doing so, we might overlook the more enduring elements of well-being: nurturing relationships, personal development and achieving a sense of accomplishment.

Many of us believe that happiness is something we'll find in the future, not something we can have right now. We always say to ourselves, 'I'll be happy when something happens,' or 'I'll be happy when I get something I want.' This way of thinking makes us keep chasing after happiness, but it always feels just out of reach, like we can never quite catch it.

It's as if we're on a long walk, seeing a beautiful hill in the distance and thinking, *I'll be happy when I get there*. But when we reach the hill, we see another one further away and we think we must reach that one to be happy. This keeps going on and on, and we never really find the happiness we're looking for because we're always looking ahead, not at what we have right now.

This is what I like to call the happiness illusion. We spend so much time and effort thinking about the future and what we need to be happy that we forget to look at our life as it is. Many things already around us can probably make us happy, but we don't see them because we're too focused on the next big thing.

The truth is, happiness isn't somewhere far away or in the future. It's in the small things that happen daily, the moments we share with friends and family, and the things we enjoy doing. We can find happiness in the here and now, not just in a future that hasn't happened yet.

Choose to focus on the real thing instead. Choose to focus on your happiness.

The next big thing is now.

Making Hard Stuff Easy: Reframing Happiness

Take five minutes to reflect on your own story and connect the dots of happiness by answering these five questions:

What does happiness mean to you?

When you think of a happy memory, what comes to mind?

On a scale from one to ten, how would you rate your personal happiness and why?

When was the last time you felt truly at peace or content, and what were you doing?

> **What small thing happened to you today that brought you happiness?**

Conditional Happiness aka the Dissatisfaction Trap

Conditional happiness happens when people think they'll only be happy if certain things occur or they get certain things they want. It's like saying to yourself, 'I'll be happy when something changes,' or 'Happiness will come when I achieve this specific goal.' This mindset makes people believe their happiness is tied to specific events or life changes, making it entirely dependent on external factors. Someone might think they'll be happy only if they can find a new job or once they've lost some weight. They place outcomes on their happiness, making it conditional on achieving these goals.

The issue with this sort of thinking is that even when people get what they have been hoping for, the feeling of happiness often doesn't last very long. For example, imagine someone finally gets the job they've been wanting. At first, they were pleased and excited. But after a while, this new job becomes just another routine, and they start looking for the next thing that will make them happy, like a higher position or more pay.

The same goes for someone who wants to lose weight. They might work hard to reach their goal and feel happy. But then the focus shifts to maintaining that weight loss and they start to worry.

If they gain a little weight, they might feel unhappy again and think they need to lose more to be happy.

This cycle of conditional happiness means that people are always looking for the next thing that will make them happy without ever finding lasting contentment. They believe that happiness comes from outside themselves – from changing their circumstances or achieving new goals.

True happiness isn't about what we have or what we achieve. It's about finding joy in the present moment and appreciating what we already have. When we stop putting conditions on our happiness, we might find that it's been there all along, waiting for us to notice it.

Be the Master of Your Happiness

To really be happy, it's essential to understand and find unconditional happiness. This is a kind of happiness that doesn't depend on what's happening in our lives or the things we have. It's about feeling content and happy inside, no matter what happens outside. This happiness stays steady and doesn't go away, even when things change.

Unconditional happiness means finding joy in who we are and what we have, not just in the things we hope to get or achieve. It's being able to smile and feel peaceful, even when things aren't perfect or when facing challenges. This type of happiness comes from within ourselves, not from outside sources.

Someone with unconditional happiness can feel happy even when it's raining and they can't go outside. They find something joyful in the sound of the rain or enjoy spending time indoors. They don't need perfect weather to feel happy. If they have a tough day at work or school, they still find reasons to be cheerful – maybe because they have a loving family or are grateful for their health.

The happiness that comes from within is powerful because it doesn't shake or disappear with life's ups and downs. It's like having a warm glowing light inside that keeps shining, even on those rainy days. To have this kind of happiness, we need to look inside ourselves, find out what makes us truly happy and focus on those things rather than always looking outside for happiness.

Unconditional happiness is about understanding that while we can't always control what happens in our lives, we can control how we react. We can find happiness in the small everyday things and be grateful for what we have. It's a happiness that's always there, quietly waiting for us to recognize and embrace it.

Making Hard Stuff Easy: How to Develop Unconditional Happiness (SPIDER)

Learning to develop unconditional happiness isn't easy. It requires a lot of repetition, practice and understanding yourself. But as with all the ideas in this book, if you're willing to do the hard stuff, you'll find that life becomes much easier.

Skill
Presence
Impermanence
Detachment
Emotion
Removal

Dig deep for lasting happiness.

S = Skill: Developing the Skill of Happiness

Happiness, much like any skill, is something you can improve with practice. You can work on it by doing activities such as meditation and gratitude journalling. Making these practices a regular part of your daily routine is essential.

Mastering Presence

Meditation is a great way to help calm your mind and bring peace to your everyday life. It's like pressing pause on the hustle and bustle that fills our days, giving your mind a chance to rest and re-energize. Just spending a few minutes on this each day can really help.

To get started, find a quiet spot where you won't be disturbed and set a five-minute timer – this is enough time to begin with. The goal here isn't to make your mind completely blank but rather to let your thoughts come and go.

Imagine your thoughts are like feathers landing softly on a box. Instead of holding on to these thoughts or getting wrapped up in the feelings they bring, picture them being gently picked up by a breeze and drifting away. Watch each thought as it floats off, not getting attached to it or dwelling on it.

This way of seeing your thoughts – as feathers caught in the wind – is crucial to meditation. If you can visualize your thoughts like this and let them go, then you're doing it right! It's a simple but effective way to practise meditation.

Don't Overthink It

Whenever I hear the word 'meditation', my mind instantly conjures the image of a Tibetan monk serenely perched for hours on a mountain's edge. Like many, I tried to embrace this practice multiple times, initially baffled by its purpose and process. I've stumbled and questioned through my journey, yet gradually, I've understood its essence.

Meditation, simply put, is the art of training your mind to acknowledge a thought and let it drift by untethered. Remember the feather analogy from before?

This is what meditation teaches us. In a world where overthinking is as natural as breathing, dedicating five minutes daily to this practice can be transformative. The peace it brings, once elusive to me, now colours my days with a calmness I never knew I was missing.

It's an invaluable skill, a quiet revolution against the chaos of our thoughts, and one that I believe is worth everyone's time to master.

Gratitude Journalling

Showing gratitude, or being thankful, is the ultimate happiness habit. It involves thinking about and appreciating the good things in your life. These can be big things, like your family and friends, or little things, like a tasty meal or a sunny day. When you focus on these positive things, it can really improve your mood and help you notice all the good around you.

To start gratitude journalling, you just need a pen and some paper. Write down these prompts and spend a few minutes thinking and writing down answers to each of them.

What is something in your home you love the most?

Think about an item in your house that brings you joy or comfort. It could be a cosy chair, a photo of a happy memory or even your favourite mug. Write down what this item is and why it means so much to you.

Think of the last place you visited that made you feel calm and peaceful.

What was it about this place that brought you such peace? Consider the scenery, quietness or personal connection that made it special.

Think about a relationship that has positively affected your life. What has it taught you about love, friendship or trust?

Reflect on a relationship that has had a good impact on your life. This could be with a family member, a friend or even a pet. Write about what this relationship has shown you about important values like love, friendship and trust.

Gratitude journalling is a powerful way to remind yourself of the good things in your life. It helps you focus on the positive, making you feel happier and more content.

Making Hard Stuff Easy: Gratitude Foundations

Take five minutes to recalibrate the way you perceive your reality and instead of stumbling deeper into the rut of negativity focus on the positives when things go wrong.

What are three things that happened to you today you are grateful for?

What is the one thing you aren't currently giving yourself credit for?

Who are you grateful for in your life and why?

What was the last accomplishment that made you proud of yourself?

What is one thing you are looking forward to this week? If it doesn't exist, plan it.

P = Presence: Enjoying the Moment You're In

Learning to enjoy the moment you're in, no matter what it brings, is all about being present. It means paying attention to what's happening now and not just thinking about what's coming next.

'Enjoy the little things, for one day you may look back and realize they were the big things'

– Robert Brault

Being present is about really noticing everything around you – the way the sun feels on your skin, the sound of birds singing or the taste of your food. It's about enjoying what you're doing now, whether walking, talking to a friend or just sitting quietly.

Sometimes, we get so caught up in waiting for the next holiday, the following weekend or the next big event that we don't notice the little things that make our everyday life so special. When you learn to be present, you start seeing how much there is to enjoy and be grateful for.

Being present means really tasting each bite of your favourite meal, smelling the aromas and appreciating the food. If you're talking to someone, it means really listening to them, not thinking about what you'll say next or what you need to do later.

Enjoying the moment you're in makes life richer and more enjoyable. It helps you appreciate the little things that make you feel more calm, happy and connected to the world.

I = Impermanence: Nothing Stays the Same Forever

Impermanence is about realizing that life and everything in it constantly changes and that nothing outside us stays the same forever. Things like our jobs, the places we live and even our relationships. Because these things constantly change, we can't depend on them to make us happy.

Impermanence is a fact of life. Flowers bloom and fade away, seasons change, and even the busiest cities can become quiet. This can be sad to think about, but it also teaches us a valuable lesson about finding happiness. It reminds us to enjoy and appreciate things while we have them but not to hold on too tightly because they won't last forever.

'We live only in the present'

– Marcus Aurelius

You might have a favourite gadget right now. It's great to enjoy it, but it's also important to remember that one day it might break or you might lose interest in it. The same goes for life experiences. Enjoy the good times, but know that they will change, and that's OK.

Understanding that life is impermanent helps us to be more flexible and less upset when things do change. It encourages us to find happiness within ourselves instead of looking for it only in things or situations that will eventually change or end. This way, we can be more at peace and find a more lasting happiness.

D = Detachment: Don't Tie Your Happiness to a Result

Detachment (the good kind) means not letting your happiness depend too much on the results or outcomes of things you want or do. It's about having hopes and dreams but not letting your inner peace and happiness be tied entirely to whether these things happen.

For example, imagine you're looking forward to a day out with friends. It's great to be excited about it, but if something changes and the day out can't happen, try not to let it make you too unhappy. Being detached means you understand that sometimes plans change, and that's all right. You find ways to be content and happy even if things don't go as planned.

This doesn't mean you shouldn't care about things or work hard for what you want. It's good to have goals and to put effort into achieving them. Detachment is more about how you handle the feelings that come with success or failure. It's about not letting these feelings control you.

'The secret of health for both mind and body is not to mourn for the past, worry about the future, or anticipate troubles, but to live in the present moment wisely and earnestly'

– Attributed to Buddha

By practising detachment, you learn to enjoy doing things rather than focusing on the end result. It helps you stay calm and balanced, no matter what life throws your way, and you'll find that happiness doesn't depend on external circumstances.

E = Emotion: Keep Calm and Carry On

Working on keeping your emotions steady means learning how to stay calm and balanced, no matter what's happening around you. It's about not letting life's good and bad times affect you too much. This doesn't mean you won't feel ecstatic or sad sometimes, but it's about not letting these feelings take over completely.

If something good happens, like winning a prize or having a great day out, it's natural to feel happy and excited. But it's important not to let this excitement make you forget about other things or take risks you wouldn't usually take.

Similarly, when something not so good happens, like you have a disagreement with a friend or a plan doesn't work out, it's OK to feel upset or disappointed. But try not to let these feelings make you too sad or stop you from enjoying other parts of your life.

Learning to manage your emotions is like being the captain of a ship in the ocean. Sometimes the sea will be calm and sometimes it will be stormy. But as the captain, you learn how to steer your ship steadily through both calm and rough waters.

By working on keeping your emotions steady, you become more resilient. This means you can handle life's ups and downs better and stay calm and happy, no matter what's happening around you. It's an essential skill for finding long-lasting happiness and peace of mind.

'Detachment is not that you own nothing;
detachment is that nothing owns you'

– Bhagavad Gita

R = Removal: Stop Relying on External Things to Make You Happy

Removal is about learning not to rely on external things, like your successes or the things you own, to make you happy. It's understanding that real happiness comes from inside you, not from the things you have or what you achieve.

It's nice to have a new phone or a fancy car, and it's great to do well in a test or at work. But these things shouldn't be the only source of your happiness. If your joy only comes from getting new things or being successful, what happens when you can't have these things any more? Your happiness might go away, too.

True joy is more than just about having stuff or winning awards. It's about the love you feel for your family and friends, the peace you get from a quiet moment alone or the fun you have playing a game or enjoying a hobby. These feelings come from inside you and don't depend on what you have or your achievements.

Finding joy in simple things, like a walk in the park, a good book or a chat with a friend, helps you understand that happiness isn't about collecting things or ticking off achievements. It's about your feelings and how you see the world.

When you stop relying on external things to make you happy, you start to enjoy life more for what it is, not what you can get from it. You find happiness in being yourself and from the world around you, not just in things or successes. This way, your happiness becomes more stable and long-lasting.

Making Hard Stuff Easy: The Ego Challenge

In a world that often expects us to look and behave in specific ways, it's easy to lose track of our uniqueness and the life experiences that have shaped us. This challenge is a brilliant way to reconnect with yourself, see beyond your appearance and value your true self and your strength.

I'd like you to take five minutes for this exercise. Take out a blank piece of paper and a pen. Think about your strengths. Things you could *brag* about if you were your own wingman or wingwoman. Don't focus on what you see as flaws or weaknesses. Laughter lines indicate joyous times, stubbornness speaks of challenges you've overcome, and your stories reflect love, loss, victories and essential life lessons.

I want you to write down five things that boost your ego:

1.

2.

3.

4.

5.

'It's not how big the house is, it's how happy the home is'

– Unknown

This may initially feel odd or unusual, but, believe me, it's an incredibly powerful exercise. Pay attention to the feelings that come up when you reread each of your strengths. Focus on your personality and looks. Remember the inner strength, resilience and beauty that you possess, which you might have overlooked because you've been too caught up in life.

This challenge is more than just about learning to love yourself; it's a journey towards deeper self-understanding. Continuously doing this will help you get to know and appreciate yourself more. It will also help you recognize how your life experiences have moulded you. Embracing this challenge is a step towards celebrating yourself more, acknowledging the amazing person you've become and reminding yourself that happiness is an inside job – and that there is plenty to be grateful for in your own self.

Notice the difference?

Notes

Principle 2

Make Peace With Your Past

The Monk and the Whispering Diary

There was once a monastery in a hidden valley, surrounded by ancient forests and soothed by gentle streams. This peaceful place was home to a monk who was always lost in deep thought, searching for understanding about life and the mind.

One day, while looking through the monastery's old books, the monk found an old diary tucked away in a dusty corner. It was called the Whispering Diary and it was known to hold the thoughts of many monks from long ago. Feeling a sudden pang of curiosity, the monk started to read.

With each page turned, the monk heard quiet voices coming from the diary. These were the worries and fears of monks who had lived before, their struggles whispering through the pages. Night after night, the monk read on, soaking up the old worries and thoughts.

At first, the monk thought these whispers were interesting, like a window into the minds of those who had sought wisdom before.

But soon, the monk noticed that the diary's whispers stirred up his worries. The old fears began to mix with the monk's present, leading him into a maze of troubled thoughts. The usually calm monk became anxious, his mind filled with a storm of voices.

Looking for help, the monk went to his mentor, an older monk known for his wisdom and peace. The elder listened carefully as the monk told him about the Whispering Diary.

The elder monk smiled wisely and said, 'The diary is like a mirror for your mind. It shows you not just the past but how you react to it. Don't use it to hold on to your worries but as a tool to understand and get past them. True peace comes from learning from these voices, not being stuck in them.'

With this newly gained understanding, the monk went back to the diary. He wrote his thoughts next to the old monks' words this time. He learned to hear the whispers not as burdens but as lessons, helping him to understand himself better.

As days turned into weeks, everyone saw how much the monk had changed. The diary, once a thing that caused unrest, was now a valued source of wisdom. The voices from the past helped the monk manage his thoughts and feelings with more clarity and peace. In the calm of the monastery, guided by the Whispering Diary, the monk found his way to inner peace. He learned to live in the moment, taking wisdom from the past without being caught in it.

And so he went on to pass the wisdom to everyone who crossed his path. Peace doesn't come from ignoring our past but from understanding and learning from it. By living in the now and reflecting on what's gone, we can find peace and wisdom in the journey through life.

The First Step to Making Peace With Your Past

In trying to make peace with our past, we often think about it over and over. At first glance, this kind of thinking – where we repeatedly mull over past events, usually in a negative way – might look like it's stopping us from getting better. But if we look closer, we see that this process can be the first step. It can lead to deeper thinking, understanding and, eventually, peace with what happened before.

Everyone has times they wish they could redo, words they wish they hadn't said and actions they regret. When we keep thinking about these things, they stay in our minds. It's easy to think these thoughts are just negative and unhelpful. But they're pointing out things from our past that we haven't fully dealt with yet, things that need our attention and healing.

This kind of thinking can kickstart a deeper dive into our feelings. The more we think about certain events or choices, the more we uncover the emotions and beliefs tied to them. This helps us spot our deepest hurts, misunderstandings and habits. Once we see these, we can start understanding their origins and positively dealing with them.

However, it's important to remember that thinking over and over about the past can be like a double-edged sword. While it can show us what parts of our lives need more attention, if we do it too much and don't do anything about it, it can lead to more stress, worry and even depression. So the aim isn't to keep thinking about the past forever but to use these thoughts as a starting point for healing.

The Rumination Cycle

The rumination cycle is when someone keeps thinking about something, usually in the wrong way, which affects how they feel. It begins with a trigger – something that happens or a thought that gets this thinking started. This might be a comment from a friend or an old memory. Next is the reaction, where the person quickly starts to feel upset or worried.

Then the person starts to think about what happened and how they feel about it. This usually means they overthink and try to work out everything about the situation. The fourth step is making the event seem more important than it might be, which can make them see things in the wrong way.

Lastly, the cycle ends with these blown-up ideas becoming strong beliefs or memories. These fixed thoughts can change how the person feels and acts, often in a bad way, making them feel stressed or anxious for a long time about what happened. Breaking this cycle can be challenging, but being aware of each step in the cycle can help you resolve these issues.

The Five-Step Rumination Cycle

Trigger

This is what starts the cycle. It can be something that happens around you or something you think of suddenly. It's like a spark that sets off your thoughts. Maybe a friend says something that catches you off guard, you don't do as well as you expected in an exam or an old photo brings back memories of a time you'd rather forget. These are all triggers that begin the cycle of rumination.

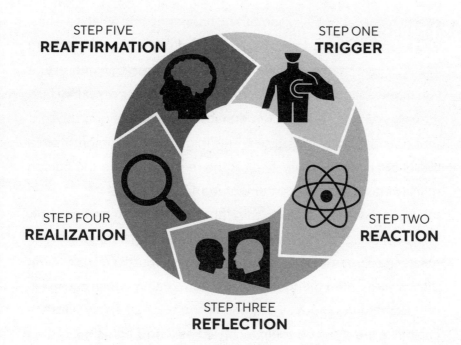

STEP FIVE
REAFFIRMATION

STEP ONE
TRIGGER

STEP FOUR
REALIZATION

STEP TWO
REACTION

STEP THREE
REFLECTION

Reaction

Right after the trigger, you have a natural response. This response can be emotional, like feeling sad or worried, or mental, where you start thinking a lot about the trigger. This reaction is your immediate way of dealing with what just happened or what you remembered. You might feel hurt or confused if a friend makes an offhand remark. Or if you remember a past mistake, you might start feeling anxious about it all over again. These feelings are your initial reactions to the trigger.

Reflection

In this stage, you start thinking more deeply about what happened. You review the event and your feelings about it, trying to make sense of them. This step involves a lot of thinking, and sometimes overthinking, about why something happened and what it means. You keep thinking about why your friend said what they did and what it might have meant. Or if you're remembering a past event, you might spend a lot of time analysing why it happened and how it made you feel, trying to understand every detail.

Realization

In this stage, the event or thought from the trigger starts to seem much more significant than it might be. You start to blow things out of proportion, thinking that a small event has huge implications or meanings. You might begin to believe that your friend's comment means your entire friendship is in trouble or that not doing well in one exam means you're not good at the subject. This realization can make the situation seem much worse than it actually is.

Reaffirmation

This is where your realized thoughts start to feel like solid truths. What might have begun as a slight worry or a simple memory now becomes a big belief or a defining memory for you. These thoughts get firmly planted in your mind and can shape how you see yourself and the world. You might become convinced that your friendship is definitely troubled because of that comment, or you might start believing that you will always struggle in a particular subject because of one bad exam. These reaffirmed thoughts can significantly impact your feelings and behaviour going forward.

From Rumination to Resolution

Making peace with our past means moving from overthinking to sorting things out. Once we know what makes us overthink, we need to face these memories, feelings or beliefs, understand how they affect us now and do something to make peace or deal with them. Each step in the rumination cycle needs us to do something and then change our approach.

The Trigger Trick

The key here is to be aware. Realize that this event, comment or memory makes you ruminate. This might not be easy at first, but you'll get better at spotting these triggers with practice. When you notice one, try not to react straight away. Take a deep breath instead. This pause can help you calm down and stop you from getting too caught up in your thoughts.

You could also write down what happened or what was said. Put it in a diary, your notes app or on a piece of paper. This way, you can look at it later when you feel calmer and ready to think about it. Writing it down also helps you step back from the situation momentarily. It's like telling yourself, *I'll deal with this, but not right this second*. This can be helpful because it allows you to break from the immediate emotions and thoughts the trigger might cause.

This is the first step in controlling the cycle of rumination. You're recognizing what sets it off and giving yourself a way to handle it better. It starts to break the automatic reaction of jumping straight into a whirlwind of thoughts.

The Reaction Resolution

Stop and take a deep breath before you get carried away by your initial reaction. Remember the meditation exercise we discussed within Principle 1 – the box and the feather?

It's important to remind yourself that the way you react at first is often shaped by things that have happened to you before. Your first feelings might not really show what's happening right now.

Try not to get stuck in these negative feelings. Instead, ask yourself helpful questions like 'What can I learn from this situation?' or 'What's a better way for me to handle this?' Questions like these can help you think more positively and find better ways to deal with what's happening.

It's also essential to create what I call The Gap. This is a short time between something happening and how you react to it. By making this gap, you give yourself a chance to think before you respond. This means you can choose to react in a better way instead of just going with your first emotion or thought.

If someone says something that upsets you, instead of immediately getting angry or upset, use The Gap to think about why they might have said it and how you can respond calmly. This could mean taking a moment to breathe deeply, counting to ten in your head or stepping away for a few minutes.

By taking this approach, you're in charge of how you respond. Instead of just going with the first emotion, you're giving yourself time to think. It's like pressing pause when you're watching a film – this break allows you to stop for a moment and think about the story. This pause can help you see things more clearly and decide on the best reaction rather than just acting on your first impulse.

The Reflection Reframe

Use this time of deep thought in a good way. It's normal to want to work out what happened but try not to let your thoughts go round and round in a harmful or ineffectual way. Try to think in a way that helps you grow. Instead of thinking about your feelings, look at the situation from every side. Maybe there was just a mix-up or

'You cannot see your reflection in boiling water. Similarly you cannot see the truth in a state of anger. When the waters calm, clarity comes'

– Unknown

maybe there's something you can learn from what happened. Try to think of ways to solve the problem or look at things differently.

I often use a way of thinking called Hanlon's Razor, which states:

'Never attribute to malice that which can be adequately explained by stupidity.'

Let me give you an example: imagine you go on a date and end up waiting for an hour. You might start thinking the person doesn't like you or that they're being rude by standing you up. But then you find out later that they turned up at a different restaurant, which had a similar name, three miles away. They weren't trying to be mean or make you feel bad; they just made a silly mistake.

In situations like this, it's easy to think the worst about the other person or even yourself. But often, it's just a simple mistake or bad luck. Remembering Hanlon's Razor can help you stop jumping to negative conclusions. It's like stepping back and asking yourself, 'Could there be a simpler, less hurtful reason for this?' This way of thinking can stop you from feeling hurt or angry about things that might not be as bad as they seem.

The Realization Resolution

Be on the lookout and watch how you think about things. If you start to see a situation as much bigger or more severe than it really was, understand that our minds can make things seem worse. If you find yourself doing this, stop and think about your thoughts. Ask yourself, 'Is this true, or am I making it out to be more than it was?'

Talking to a friend or someone you trust about how you see things can be beneficial. They might be able to give you a different view of the situation, one that's truer to what happened, which can help you get a more balanced and fair understanding of the event.

A great technique to use is what I call 'the friend's lens'. Here's how it works.

Write down what happened as if you're telling someone else about it. Then imagine that a friend has just told you this story and is asking you for advice. Think about what you would say to them. Often, the advice we would give to someone else is exactly what we need to hear ourselves. The important thing is to then start using that advice in your own life. This approach can help you to be kinder and more understanding of yourself, seeing the situation in a more reasonable and balanced way, just like you would if a friend came to you with the same problem.

The Reaffirmation Refresh

Before you let a big belief take root in your mind, stop and think about whether it's really true. Ask yourself if this belief is built on actual facts or just guesses you're making. Sometimes, these beliefs come more from things that happened to us in the past rather than what's going on right now. It's essential to check whether your thoughts are about the here and now or are being coloured by old experiences.

Try doing things that go against these stuck beliefs. This can help you see if they're really true. For example, if you start thinking you're not good at your job because of one mistake, try taking on new tasks at work. This can show you that one mistake doesn't define your skills or worth. It's like testing your belief to see if it holds up. You might discover that you're much more capable than you thought, which can help break down those untrue beliefs.

Challenging beliefs with actions allows you to see things more clearly and learn that you're capable of more than you might have thought. It's like shining a light on a shadow – the scary shape you thought you saw often turns out to be much less frightening when you look at it properly.

Making Hard Stuff Easy: From Rumination to Resolution

Use the table below to get yourself out of a rumination cycle or a thought pattern that's keeping you from achieving your goals. Name the trigger, identify your reaction, put it through the friend's lens and then decide whether you want to enforce it or get rid of it.

The Trigger What triggered you to start ruminating on the past?	
The Reaction What was your initial reaction to the trigger? How did you respond?	
The Reflection How did this trigger make you feel for the rest of the day? Did it cause you to overthink and make up scenarios in your head?	

The Realization Is your train of thought helping or hindering you? Do you need to adjust how you think of this trigger and address the underlying issues behind it?	
Reaffirmation What needs to change here to stop this rumination cycle from happening again?	

Making Hard Stuff Easy: Reversing the Cycle

The hard stuff in making peace with your past is identifying your current triggers and how they ended up turning into solid truths in your head. Below, I've listed two examples of how this can occur with relationships and weight loss and what steps to take to reverse the cycle.

Reversing the Cycle of Relationships – James's Story

James had been in a relationship with Alex for three years. They seemed happy until the day James discovered Alex was cheating on him. When confronted, Alex cruelly said they didn't find James attractive any more. This comment deeply hurt James, and he couldn't shake the feeling of being unattractive.

Over time, James repeatedly thought about Alex's words. He reflected on them excessively, thinking that it must be true if someone he loved could say this. He magnified this belief, thinking that he was not only unattractive to Alex but also to everyone. This thought became a 'solid truth' in his mind.

As a result, James struggled to find and maintain new relationships. He believed he was not worthy of love and that anyone he dated would eventually see him as unattractive. This belief, rooted in a past experience, overshadowed his interactions and made him fearful of commitment and intimacy.

To reverse this cycle, James needs to understand that the trigger – Alex's infidelity and hurtful comment – was more about Alex's issues than his own worth or attractiveness. He needs to recognize that Alex's cheating and subsequent blaming were due to their own insecurities, low self-esteem and inability to communicate honestly. It was an unfair deflection of their guilt on to James.

James needs to see that this one person's actions and words don't define his worth or desirability. By understanding that the problem was with Alex and not with him, James can dismantle the false belief that he is unattractive and unworthy of love.

He can start challenging this belief by seeking out experiences that reinforce his desirability and worthiness of love, engaging in new social activities, meeting new people and showing that he deserves love and a stable, fulfilling relationship.

This process involves James actively questioning the validity of his long-held belief and replacing it with a healthier, more accurate view of himself. By doing so, he can open himself up to the possibility of love and connection in a way his rumination cycle had previously blocked.

Reversing the Cycle of Weight Loss - Sam's Story

Sam had participated in an extreme weight loss programme and had lost a staggering 40lbs in three months. The transformation was so dramatic that Sam became a poster person for the programme. However, the methods used were intense and unsustainable. Once the programme ended, Sam gradually returned to normal eating habits and regained 40lbs.

This weight gain made Sam feel guilty and like a failure. They believed they had let down the programme and themselves. This feeling of failure became a 'solid truth' in Sam's mind. As a result, every time Sam tried to start a new weight loss journey, they would end up sabotaging their efforts, driven by a deep fear of success and the pressure of potentially letting others down again.

To reverse this cycle, Sam needs to understand that the problem wasn't with them but with the extreme nature of the weight loss programme. Rapid weight loss methods often don't offer sustainable long-term results or teach healthy lifelong habits. Sam must recognize that the programme's unrealistic standards and practices are at fault for creating a distorted view of weight loss and maintenance.

Sam can start by acknowledging that sustainable weight loss is a gradual process and involves building healthy long-term habits rather than seeking immediate, drastic results. They need to forgive themselves for the weight regain and understand that it's an expected outcome with such extreme weight loss methods.

Engaging in a more balanced approach to weight loss, focusing on nourishing the body and developing a healthy relationship with food and exercise can help Sam break free from the cycle of self-sabotage. Seeking support from others who understand sustainable weight management can also aid this journey.

By shifting the perspective from blaming themselves to understanding the flawed approach of the extreme programme, Sam can begin to heal their relationship with their body and with food. This involves dismantling the belief that they are a failure and replacing it with the understanding that proper health and weight management is about balance, self-care and sustainable lifestyle changes.

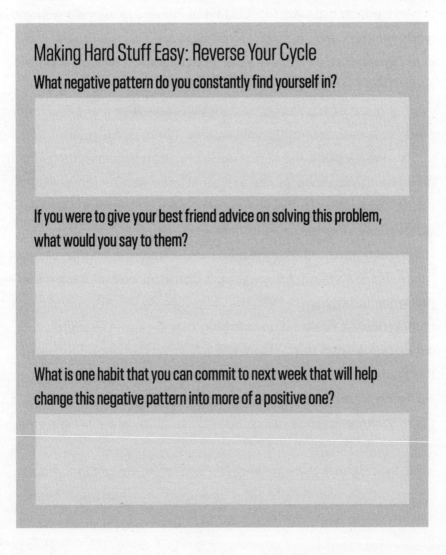

Making Hard Stuff Easy: Reverse Your Cycle

What negative pattern do you constantly find yourself in?

If you were to give your best friend advice on solving this problem, what would you say to them?

What is one habit that you can commit to next week that will help change this negative pattern into more of a positive one?

The Art of Letting Go

Dealing with past regrets, bad feelings and old hurts often feels like a hefty load that keeps dragging you down. But the great thing about taking a good hard look inside yourself is that it can liberate you from these burdens, starting you on a path towards feeling free and light.

Learning to let go focuses on this process of becoming free. When we face our past troubles head-on and genuinely get to grips with them, we begin the process of healing. This can happen in many ways: maybe by talking things through with someone, taking time to really think things over, saying sorry to ourselves or others, or just accepting things that have happened and can't be changed. This journey helps to refresh and renew our spirit.

This isn't just about sorting out our thoughts and feelings, though. It also leads to fundamental physical changes. Our emotions, especially old and deep-seated ones, can become lodged in our bodies, getting stuck in our muscles and joints.

Physical activities like yoga, dancing or regular exercise can help release these hidden emotions. This release supports not only our emotional well-being but also our overall health and wellness. When we finally let go, we do more than come to terms with our past. We also open ourselves up to a present and a future that's lighter, full of freedom and rich with possibilities. This way, we finally make peace with our past and move forward into a brighter, more hopeful future.

Making Hard Stuff Easy: Find Your Why (And Get Rid of It)

Grab a pen and paper and write down a recurring problem.

The primary goal of this challenge is to help you dig deep and find the root cause of this problem instead of the surface-level answers you've been giving yourself.

Here's an example so you understand the process of this challenge:

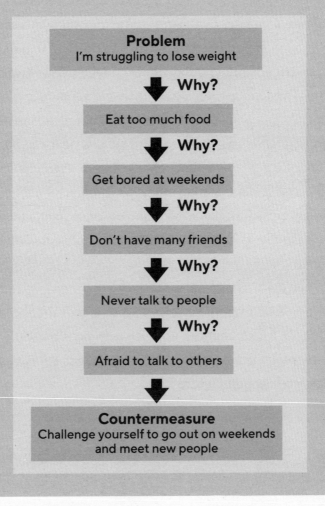

Problem
I'm struggling to lose weight

Why?

Eat too much food

Why?

Get bored at weekends

Why?

Don't have many friends

Why?

Never talk to people

Why?

Afraid to talk to others

Countermeasure
Challenge yourself to go out on weekends and meet new people

As you can see from the example, this person's problem with weight loss is the boredom of staying in every weekend eating food on the sofa and not interacting with others. It can be scary to put yourself out there and meet new people, which is why so many people avoid doing so. Still, when you finally build the courage to do the hard stuff, you'll have an easier life.

Start with the problem at the top of the paper, then write five whys down the page. When you've answered the whys, devise the countermeasure that you will action to resolve them.

Problem

Why 1

Why 2

Why 3

Why 4

Why 5

The Big Countermeasure

MAKE PEACE WITH YOUR PAST | 77

Notes

Principle 3

Love Yourself

The Midsummer Song

Deep in far-away mountains lay an enchanted forest, humming and alive with nightingales that sang their melodies. Among them was a young nightingale with messy feathers and a song as sweet as the morning dew. From an early age, his existence was filled with music. His mother's voice could warm the coldest morning. His father could make the leaves dance with his melodies. For them, music was the essence of life itself. He knew they were all part of something bigger. He also knew he was talented. Still, as he listened to the music of other nightingales, he couldn't stop the bitter feelings of jealousy and comparison from creeping up on him.

Determined to find his spotlight, he practised tirelessly, often until the moon climbed high into the night sky, striving to outsing the rest. One evening, after a particularly strenuous rehearsal, he perched alone in a secluded grove, his throat aching and his spirit low. His song seemed to mock him, echoing his fears of never emerging from the shadow of the enchanted woods.

Overwhelmed, he wept into the night, contemplating silence over song. At that moment, the grove's silence was broken by a wise old owl. She overheard the nightingale's sobbing and, moved by the depth of his emotion, asked, 'What troubles you, little nightingale?'

Through teary eyes, the nightingale shared his woes. 'No matter how hard I try, I can't outshine the others. I'll always be just another voice lost in the crowd,' he chirped, his voice quivering.

The wise owl perched beside him, her gaze soft and understanding. 'Song, my little nightingale, isn't merely about talent. It's about emotion, the stories we tell, and the hearts we touch with our melodies. When you sing from your soul, you reach others in ways that mere skill cannot.'

'But I'm always compared to others,' the nightingale sighed, his heart heavy.

The wise owl drew herself up tall. 'Comparison is the nature of observers, but remember, each bird's song is unique. Brimming with passion, your voice will resonate with those who hear it. It's not about being the best; it's about staying true to yourself.'

Comforted by these words, the nightingale realized his fear of comparison had made him forget the joy of singing.

The woods were abuzz with anticipation when the time came for the midsummer concert. The little nightingale, taking his place under the moon's spotlight, felt a hush fall over the woods. Closing his eyes, he inhaled deeply and began his song.

This time, it was unlike any before. He wasn't just performing; he was singing from the heart. As his final note lingered in the cool night air, the entire forest held its breath, only to erupt into cheers. The nightingale felt warmth spill inside him. He realized that despite how amazing it felt to be praised and admired, that wasn't what truly mattered; it was his love for music that did. And so from that night on, he continued to enchant the forest and its visitors with songs as sweet as the morning dew, his own voice being the only one he compared himself with.

The Self-Love Crisis

In late 2020, a study was done in twenty-one countries to discover how people view themselves. Over 22,000 people aged eighteen and over were interviewed. The study focused on self-love and looked at how people see themselves, how often they feel nervous or anxious, their confidence, their ability to bounce back and what makes them feel good about themselves.

They used the information from the study to create a Global Self-Love Index. This index gives people a score from zero to a hundred, ranging from lots of self-doubt to complete self-love.

Self-Love Index

Low Self-Love   **High Self-Love**

The results showed that many people around the world are struggling with self-love. The average score on the self-love index was only fifty-three out of a hundred. About half the people scored on the lower side of the scale, feeling more self-doubt than self-love.

Six out of ten people worldwide said they wished they respected themselves more, and four out of ten sometimes felt they are not useful. More than half the people admitted that they often pretend to be happy to make others happy, even if they don't feel happy themselves, hiding their real feelings from those around them.

The Importance of Self-Love

Loving yourself truly helps you realize your value, which is crucial to becoming more confident. When you have a lot of self-love, you don't depend on others to feel good about yourself. This lets you enter relationships feeling solid and confident, not just seeking approval from someone else.

Self-love is about wholeheartedly accepting yourself just as you are. It involves being kind and gentle with yourself, just like you would be with a close friend. This kind of love is not only about treating yourself well, like exercising regularly and getting plenty of sleep, but it also includes how you think and feel about yourself internally.

When you love yourself, you generally view yourself in a positive way. This doesn't mean that you must always feel happy with yourself – that's not possible or realistic. We all have days when we feel down or are hard on ourselves. There might be times when I'm frustrated or upset with myself. Maybe I made a mistake or didn't meet my own expectations. Even during these moments, I still maintain a sense of love for myself. The best way to look at this is to compare it to how we love others.

Take, for instance, how you might love a family member like a child. You can love your child deeply, yet there might be times when you feel annoyed or let down by their actions. Perhaps they didn't do well at school or broke something. Even in these moments, your love for them doesn't waver. This love means you

'There is nothing noble about being superior to some other man. The true nobility is in being superior to your previous self'

– Hindu Proverb

forgive them, try to understand why they acted the way they did, ensure their needs are met and guide them to make better choices in the future. Loving yourself works in much the same way. If you can show others this level of understanding and compassion, you can show it to yourself.

Self-love is an ongoing process. It's about being patient with yourself, understanding your emotions, recognizing your needs and making decisions that benefit your well-being. It's a nurturing and forgiving love that acknowledges your flaws and imperfections. Doing so creates a supportive inner world that helps you thrive and grow, even when you face challenges or make mistakes.

In the story at the beginning of the chapter, we see the process of learning to love ourselves. Even though you may compare yourself with others and doubt your own abilities, you can learn to accept and love your unique skills. The young nightingale's story teaches us that self-love isn't about being better than others or perfect. It's about recognizing and appreciating our unique qualities. Like the nightingale, we can start to shine when we learn to see and love what makes us different. On our journey to self-love, it is important that we learn to accept and value ourselves, because that's when we can reach our full potential.

The Five Components of Self-Love

The road to fostering self-love is based on five components, each as important as the next: self-compassion, self-awareness, self-care, self-acceptance and healthy boundaries.

Self-Compassion

Self-compassion is about being kind to yourself, particularly when things don't go your way or you face challenging times. It means not being too hard on yourself or overly critical when you make a mistake or fail at something. Imagine how you'd treat a good friend having a hard time – that's the kind of understanding and care you should show yourself. (Remember the friend's lens!)

When you practise self-compassion, you acknowledge that everyone makes mistakes and faces challenges. It's a normal part of being human. Instead of getting upset with yourself or feeling like you're not good enough, recognize that it's OK not to be perfect. You give yourself the comfort and encouragement needed to get through rough patches.

Being self-compassionate also means you don't constantly judge yourself harshly. You understand that setbacks are opportunities to learn and grow, not just reasons to feel bad about yourself. You know to be your own supporter, giving yourself pep talks and positive reinforcement.

This approach can change how you handle stress and challenges. High self-compassion makes you more likely to pick yourself up after a setback and try again. You'll find that you're more resilient and better able to cope with life's ups and downs.

In everyday life, self-compassion can show up in small ways. It might be taking a break when you're feeling overwhelmed, speaking kindly to yourself when you make a mistake or simply giving yourself permission to relax and do something enjoyable. It's about treating yourself with the same kindness, care and understanding you would offer to someone you care about.

Making Hard Stuff Easy: The Time-Travel Challenge

I want you to spend five minutes thinking about a tough time or when you made a mistake. This challenge aims to help you be kinder to yourself, especially when you remember times you found hard or felt not good enough. By supporting your past self, you learn to be just as kind and understanding to yourself now. This task helps you connect past mistakes or hurts with what you know now and shows you that everyone changes and gets better over time.

Picture yourself travelling back in time as the person you are today and meeting your past self during that difficult period. What advice and comforting words would you give? How could you show support and understanding? Jot down these thoughts here in the space provided or say them out loud.

Self-Awareness

Self-awareness is about knowing and understanding your feelings, your needs and wants, and your strengths and weaknesses. It's like having a clear map of your emotions and thoughts. This understanding can be improved by doing things like meditation and journalling.

When you are more self-aware, you better understand why you feel a certain way or react to things the way you do. It's like being a detective of your mind – you get to understand what makes you tick. This can help you make better choices in life because you know what's truly important to you and what isn't.

Meditation is one way to boost self-awareness. When you meditate, you spend time quietly with your thoughts, which can help you notice patterns in your thinking or how certain thoughts make you feel. This can lead to a deeper understanding of yourself.

Journalling is another excellent way to develop your self-awareness. When you write down your thoughts and feelings, it's easier to see them. You might notice things about yourself that you didn't realize before. Writing out your thoughts and feelings is a great way of reflecting on and learning from your experiences.

By becoming more self-aware, you can better manage your emotions, understand your relationships and make decisions that align with who you are. It's like having an inner guide who helps you navigate through life with more confidence and understanding.

Making Hard Stuff Easy: Hack Your Triggers

Choose a day this week to try out this challenge. During the day, watch for anything or anyone that annoys you or gets on your nerves. If something like this happens, make a quick note of it. You don't need to think about it too much at the time – but write it down so you can look at it later.

Go through everything you've written down. Look at each thing that bothered you, what happened and how you felt when it did. Spend some time thinking about what caused these feelings. Were they responses to things happening around you? Reactions to people? Or were they influenced by your thoughts and views? This challenge aims to help you become more aware of yourself. It's about understanding how what happens outside and inside (your thoughts) can affect how you feel.

What was the trigger?

How did you respond?

Why did it trigger you?

How will you respond to it next time?

The Trigger Hack	
The Trigger	
The Reaction	
The Reason	
Your Next-Time Reaction	

Self-Care

Self-care is purposefully doing things to look after your body, mind and emotions. It's taking steps to make sure you're healthy and happy. This can be as simple as enjoying a relaxing bath, calling a friend for support or ensuring you're getting enough sleep.

Self-care means recognizing what you need to feel good and taking action to meet those needs. It's like giving yourself a helping hand to stay well. This could be exercising to keep your body strong, eating healthy foods or finding time to do things you enjoy, like reading a book or walking.

It also involves looking after your mental health. This might mean stepping away from stressful situations when needed or talking about your feelings with friends, family or a professional. It's about finding healthy ways to deal with stress, anxiety or sadness.

Taking care of your emotional well-being is also a big part of self-care. This could include practising meditation or mindfulness or just doing things that make you happy. It's about understanding your emotions and finding healthy ways to express and deal with them.

It's easy to forget to look after yourself in a busy world. Still, self-care is essential for staying healthy and happy. It doesn't have to be complicated or take a lot of time. Even small acts of self-care, like taking a few deep breaths or having a cup of tea, can make a big difference. Remember, taking care of yourself isn't selfish – it's necessary for a balanced and fulfilling life.

Making Hard Stuff Easy: The Perfect Day Challenge

Imagine having an entire day all to yourself, entirely dedicated to self-care, with no external demands or interruptions. It's a day for you to do whatever makes you feel good.

Start by thinking about or writing down how you would spend this day. What activities would you include that make you feel most relaxed, rejuvenated and genuinely happy? Consider the things that bring your life a sense of calm and joy. Would you start the day with a peaceful walk, indulge in a favourite hobby or perhaps read a book you've wanted to?

Consider how you would cater to your physical, mental and emotional well-being. This might involve doing some exercise you enjoy, practising relaxation techniques like meditation or yoga, or engaging in creative activities like painting or writing. Would you cook a healthy meal, take a long bath or spend time in nature?

Also, reflect on how you'd look after your emotional health. Would you journal your thoughts, listen to your favourite music or spend some time reflecting?

This exercise aims to help you identify the self-care activities that genuinely resonate with you. By imagining your perfect day, you gain insight into the practices most beneficial for your overall well-being. This can guide you in incorporating these activities into your routine, helping to ensure that you regularly take time for yourself and your needs.

Plan Your Perfect Day

How You'd Start It	
How You'd End It	
For Physical Well-Being	
For Mental Well-Being	
For Emotional Well-Being	
Guilty Pleasure of the Day	
Something You Would Get Rid Of	

Self-Acceptance

Self-acceptance means fully embracing every part of yourself, even those parts you might think of as flaws or imperfections. It's about understanding that nobody is perfect and accepting yourself just as you are.

When you practise self-acceptance, you stop being hard on yourself for not being perfect. Instead, you start to see your so-called flaws as another part of your uniqueness. It's like looking in the mirror and appreciating yourself for who you are instead of focusing on what you don't like.

Self-acceptance isn't about giving up on trying to improve or grow. It's about acknowledging your current state and being OK with it. For example, you might want to get fitter or learn a new skill, and that's great, but at the same time you accept and respect yourself as you are right now.

Making mistakes and having weaknesses is a normal part of life. Everyone has things they're not so good at, and that's OK. It's about embracing your whole self – the good, the bad and everything in between.

Learning to accept yourself can have a significant impact on your overall well-being. It can make you feel more confident, reduce stress and improve your mental health. When you're OK with who you are, you're more likely to be happier and more at peace with yourself.

In everyday life, self-acceptance shows up when you stop comparing yourself to others, are kind to yourself and don't let your inner critic be too harsh. It's about giving yourself the same kindness and understanding you'd give a friend.

Making Hard Stuff Easy: The Mirror Challenge

Find a mirror and stand in front of it. I want you to spend five minutes just looking at your reflection. I want you to observe yourself without any judgement or negative thoughts.

During this time, try to identify at least three things about yourself that you genuinely appreciate and feel proud of. These could be physical features you admire, personality traits you're proud of, achievements you've accomplished or even challenges you've successfully overcome. Take a moment to acknowledge the significance of each. Say out loud why each one is a

valuable and integral part of who you are. It could be your smile that you find welcoming, your sense of humour that brightens the day for others or the resilience you showed during a difficult time.

The aim here is to notice these positive aspects and feel a sense of pride and gratitude for them. This exercise is designed to shift your focus from self-criticism to self-appreciation. By recognizing and voicing what you value in yourself, you build a more positive and loving relationship with yourself.

Doing this challenge regularly can be a powerful tool in cultivating a more balanced and positive view of yourself. It encourages you to look at yourself with kindness and acceptance, a crucial step towards self-love and well-being.

How hard was this exercise, on a scale from one to ten?

/ 10

How good do you feel about yourself, on a scale from one to ten?

/ 10

On average, do you feel like you don't give yourself enough credit?

What were the things you noticed in yourself?

Repeat this exercise regularly and notice the difference.

Healthy Boundaries

Healthy boundaries are about understanding and setting limits on what you find acceptable in how others treat you and what you're willing to put up with in different parts of your life. It's like drawing a line that marks what does and doesn't sit well with you.

Setting these boundaries means knowing where you stand on things like your personal space, time, emotions and values. For example, it could be telling someone you need some time alone, saying no to extra work when you're already too busy or not allowing others to speak disrespectfully.

Healthy boundaries help you maintain your well-being and respect. They are not about being selfish or rude; instead, they're about taking care of yourself. It's essential to communicate your boundaries clearly to others. This helps people understand what you're comfortable with and how they can respect your needs.

These boundaries can also change depending on the situation or your relationship with someone. For instance, what you share with a close friend might differ from what you share with a colleague. It's about knowing what feels right for you in different situations.

Healthy boundaries are also about respecting other people's limits. Just like you have your boundaries, others have theirs, too. Recognizing and respecting these limits helps build stronger, healthier relationships. Remember, it's OK to look after your needs and ask others to respect your boundaries.

Making Hard Stuff Easy: The Boundaries Challenge

In this task, I'd like you to think about and write down one crucial rule for each of these three areas: your physical, mental and emotional well-being. We will call those your *three non-negotiables*.

Physical Boundary: pick one rule you won't compromise on for your physical health. This could be deciding how much to work so you can rest enough, doing a certain amount of exercise each week or choosing what to eat to keep your body healthy.

Mental Boundary: choose a rule for your mental health that you'll stick to. This might be setting specific times for work and your personal life to stop yourself from getting too tired, limiting how much news or social media you look at if it makes you feel bad or finding time every day for things that help clear your mind and lower stress.

Emotional Boundary: decide on a rule for looking after your emotional health. This might mean making clear rules about how others should treat you, having time to look after your feelings or choosing to spend time with people and do things that are good for your emotional state.

The goal of this challenge is to set and stick to these essential boundaries for your physical, mental and emotional health. These non-negotiables give you a way to protect your overall well-being, which helps you make better choices and deal with what life throws at you.

Name the three non-negotiables you are going to stick to this week:

The Physical Health Boundary	
The Mental Health Boundary	
The Emotional Health Boundary	

How well did you protect each of those boundaries on a scale from one to ten?

The Physical Health Boundary   / 10

The Mental Health Boundary   / 10

The Emotional Health Boundary   / 10

Making Hard Stuff Easy: Prioritizing Your Self-Care; the Six Pillars of Self-Care

Self-care encompasses a range of practices and habits across different areas of our lives, ensuring that we maintain not just physical health but also emotional, mental, spiritual, social and professional well-being. To truly thrive, it's essential to understand and implement self-care strategies in all these areas.

Let's explore the six elements of self-care, each focusing on a different aspect of our well-being:

1. **Physical Self-Care:** this involves taking care of our bodies through exercise, nutrition, adequate sleep, relaxation and regular medical check-ups. Keeping our bodies healthy and energized is the foundation of overall well-being.

2. **Emotional Self-Care:** emotional self-care is about managing our emotions effectively. This includes understanding our feelings, setting healthy boundaries, engaging in positive self-talk and connecting with others.

3. **Mental Self-Care:** here, we focus on practices that maintain and improve our mental health, like mindfulness, continuous learning, taking breaks and managing screen time and stimulants.

4. **Spiritual Self-Care:** spiritual self-care might involve meditation, spending time in nature, engaging in religious or spiritual practices or gratitude journalling to connect with our inner selves and find deeper meaning.

5. **Social Self-Care:** this is about nurturing relationships, engaging in community activities, communicating

effectively and setting boundaries in social contexts to foster a sense of belonging and support.

6. **Professional Self-Care:** professional self-care is crucial for career satisfaction and growth. It includes maintaining a work–life balance, continuous learning, taking regular breaks at work and seeking constructive feedback.

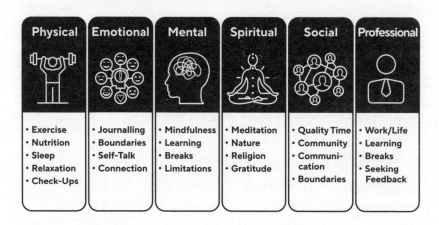

Physical	Emotional	Mental	Spiritual	Social	Professional
• Exercise • Nutrition • Sleep • Relaxation • Check-Ups	• Journalling • Boundaries • Self-Talk • Connection	• Mindfulness • Learning • Breaks • Limitations	• Meditation • Nature • Religion • Gratitude	• Quality Time • Community • Communi-cation • Boundaries	• Work/Life • Learning • Breaks • Seeking Feedback

Building the Pillar of Your Physical Self-Care

- **Regular Exercise:** whether going for a walk, attending a gym class or practising yoga, regular exercise is essential for maintaining health and reducing stress.

- **Nutrition:** eating a balanced diet with whole foods, staying hydrated and being mindful of caffeine and alcohol intake.

- **Sleep:** prioritizing quality sleep and maintaining a consistent sleep schedule.

- **Rest and Relaxation:** this might include taking short breaks during work, having a day off or just engaging in activities that relax you.

- **Check-Ups:** visits to the doctor, dentist, optician and other healthcare professionals when needed.

Building the Pillar of Your Emotional Self-Care

- **Journalling:** understanding and managing your emotions through techniques like journalling or mindfulness.
- **Boundaries:** setting healthy boundaries ensures you're not emotionally drained or overly stressed.
- **Positive Self-Talk:** challenging and reframing negative thoughts about yourself.
- **Connection:** spending time with loved ones or engaging in social activities that uplift you.

Building the Pillar of Your Mental Self-Care

- **Mindfulness:** practices that ground you and bring your attention to the present.
- **Continuous Learning:** engaging in activities that challenge and stimulate the mind, such as reading, puzzles or learning a new skill.
- **Breaks:** taking short breaks, especially during intensive tasks, to rejuvenate the mind.
- **Limiting Stimulants and Screen Time:** be mindful of caffeine intake and reduce excessive screen time, especially before bedtime.

Building the Pillar of Your Spiritual Self-Care

- **Meditation and Reflection:** spending time in silence, introspection or guided meditation to connect with your inner self.
- **Nature:** spending time outdoors, whether walking in a park, hiking or simply sitting on a beach or by a river.

- **Religious or Spiritual Practices:** engaging in rituals, prayers or other practices that align with your beliefs.
- **Gratitude Journalling:** take a moment to jot down things you're grateful for daily.

Building the Pillar of Your Social Self-Care

- **Quality Time:** spending time with friends, family or loved ones.
- **Community Engagement:** being part of a group or community, whether a club, religious group or voluntary organization.
- **Communication:** discuss feelings, thoughts or concerns openly with someone you trust.
- **Boundaries:** recognizing when to say no or when to take time for oneself.

Building the Pillar of Your Professional Self-Care

- **Work-Life Balance:** ensuring you have time outside work to relax and pursue other interests.
- **Continuous Learning:** seeking opportunities to learn and grow in your profession.
- **Breaks:** taking regular breaks during the workday to reduce stress and increase productivity.
- **Seeking Feedback:** constructive feedback can help in personal and professional growth.

The journey of self-care is unique and deeply personal. Individuals must discover what works best for them, as no one-size-fits-all approach exists.

Self-care lies in tuning in to your own needs, both physical and emotional, and responding to them with kindness and understanding. It enhances your well-being and empowers you to live a more balanced, contented and fulfilling life. Moreover, establishing a self-care plan is fundamental to learning to love yourself. Consciously choose activities and practices that nourish you and make time for them daily.

Prioritizing your well-being is a powerful expression of self-love. It reinforces the idea that you are worthy of care and attention and that taking time for yourself is necessary and deeply rewarding.

Your commitment to self-care is a commitment to yourself, one of the most important commitments you can make.

Making Hard Stuff Easy: Build Your Self-Care Plan

Commit to one thing you will incorporate this week to boost each pillar of self-care.

Physical Self-Care	
Emotional Self-Care	
Mental Self-Care	
Spiritual Self-Care	
Social Self-Care	
Professional Self-Care	

Notes

Principle 4

No One Cares

The Moonlit Dance

In the heart of the forest, where secrets were whispered through the leaves and the moon bathed everything in its soft light, there was a shy rabbit. This little rabbit was always on edge, thinking that the forest and its creatures were always watching and judging every hop it made. Every year, the animals would come together for the moonlit dance when the full moon was at its brightest. It was a night filled with magic, when the air buzzed with excitement and the forest seemed alive with joy. But the rabbit had never joined in. The fear of messing up and being laughed at kept it hiding in the shadows.

One evening, as the moon began its climb into the night sky, weaving silver paths through the trees, the rabbit sat on its own, longing to be part of the dance but trapped by its fears. That's when an old bear, known for its wisdom and understanding of the forest's deepest secrets, came over.

'Why are you sitting here all by yourself, rabbit?' the bear asked, its voice as gentle as the night air.

'I'm scared,' the rabbit muttered. 'Scared of tripping over, scared of being laughed at. If I join the dance, everyone will be looking at me.'

The bear gave a knowing nod and beckoned the rabbit to follow. They sneaked to a hidden spot, a quiet hill that looked down on the clearing where the moonlit dance was about to begin. From their secret vantage point, the rabbit watched in wonder as the forest's animals gathered. Badgers banged on hollow logs, birds moved together in perfect sync and deer twirled gracefully. Every animal was lost in their own movement, dancing freely without care.

'Take a good look, rabbit,' the bear whispered. 'Do you see anyone watching or judging? Or are they all just enjoying the moment?'

The rabbit looked carefully and realized something important. The animals were too caught up in their own fun to worry about what the others were doing. Any mistake was met with laughter – not mean but the kind that said, 'It's all good fun.' The forest wasn't a place of judgement but a space for being yourself.

Feeling a rush of bravery, the rabbit stepped into the clearing. Its heart thumped as it began to hop slowly. But as it moved, it felt the forest's rhythm take over, and its worries melted away under the moonlight.

The rabbit danced like never before, hopping and twisting. There were no judging eyes; everyone was just another dancer in the forest. In the magic of the moonlit dance, the rabbit didn't just find joy; it discovered true freedom.

As dawn approached and the dance wound down, the rabbit realized it had changed. It wasn't the timid creature it had once been but was now a true forest dweller, bold and free.

From that night onwards, the rabbit was always at the forest get-togethers, each dance a reminder of its journey to freedom. The forest's animals started to see it not as the shy rabbit but as the one who danced joyfully in the moonlight.

The rabbit realized that when we let go of worrying about what others think, we free ourselves to be who we really are and to go through life without holding back.

The Spotlight Effect

The spotlight effect describes how people tend to believe that others are paying more attention to them than they actually are, meaning we feel like we're constantly in the spotlight.

Imagine being on a stage with a spotlight on you, which makes you believe that everyone is watching and judging everything you do. You might feel like you're constantly being watched or that people are always noticing what you're wearing, how you're acting or even the small mistakes you make. It's like you're the main character in a show and the audience is always focusing on you.

We feel this way because we always think about ourselves – what we're doing, how we look and what others might think of us. This makes us believe that since we're so focused on ourselves, others must be, too. But that's not how it works. Other people are often just as focused on themselves and not on us.

In 2000, a study showed us a lot about the spotlight effect. In this experiment, a group of university students were tasked by researchers to carry out a set of unrelated tasks. Some of these students were asked to wear a T-shirt that had Barry Manilow on it. Back then, wearing a Barry Manilow T-shirt was probably one of the most embarrassing things you could do as a student.

After they finished their tasks, the students who had worn the T-shirts had to guess how many people in the room noticed what they were wearing. They estimated that about 50 per cent of students had seen their T-shirt and maybe thought it was a bit silly or embarrassing.

What was really interesting is that when they asked the other students in the room if they noticed the T-shirt, only 25 per cent said they remembered seeing it. That means the students wearing the T-shirt thought many more people noticed it than actually did.

This study shows us that we often think people are paying more attention to us than they really are. The students wearing the T-shirt felt everyone must have noticed and perhaps judged them for it. In reality, most people in the room didn't pay much attention to it or didn't think it was a big deal.

The spotlight effect dramatically impacts how we behave and feel. It's not just about feeling uncomfortable when we're around other people. The feeling of being watched all the time can make us scared to try new things or share our thoughts.

When we're worried about what other people might think, we might not do what we want to. For example, if you have a good idea in a meeting but are scared that others might not like it, you might stay quiet. Alternatively, you might really want to go to a party or a social event, but the worry that others might judge what you wear or how you act can stop you from going.

This fear of being judged or embarrassed can mean we miss out on many opportunities. We might not try a new hobby, make new friends or even go for a promotion at work. It's like a little voice in our head constantly worrying about what others will think, which holds us back. If we always think we're being judged, it's hard to

*'No one can make you feel inferior
without your consent'*

– Attributed to Eleanor Roosevelt

feel good about ourselves. We might start to doubt our ideas and abilities, which can stop us from reaching our full potential.

The spotlight effect is more than feeling awkward around other people. It's about how this feeling can stop us from doing things that might benefit us or make us happy. Understanding this can help us worry less about others' opinions and be braver in our choices.

The first step to getting past this is to really understand what the spotlight effect is. We need to remember that most people don't pay as much attention to us as we think they do. Most people are thinking about themselves, not judging us. When we start to believe this, we can begin to feel less worried about what others might think. This can help us to be more confident and less afraid to try new things and go to new places.

Once we know that people are not always watching or thinking about us, we can start to let go of our fears. We can feel more relaxed about joining in on conversations, going to social events and trying out new things. This doesn't mean we'll never feel nervous again, but it does mean we can start to enjoy being with others more and worry less. Remember, just like you're thinking about yourself, others are probably doing the same and not focusing on you.

What is the spotlight you get caught up in?

Making Hard Stuff Easy: The Role-Reversal Exercise

This exercise is all about understanding how people think in social situations. It's pretty simple: if you are thinking about something, other people are likely thinking about similar things. This means they are probably not thinking about you.

How to Do the Exercise

Notice Your Thoughts: pay attention to your thoughts next time you're around other people. Are you worried about what others think of you?

Consider Others: remember that most people probably think similar things about themselves. They're likely not focusing on you.

Feel More Relaxed: use this thought to help you relax and feel more comfortable in social situations. It can take some of the pressure off when you realize that others are not judging you as much as you might think.

Practise Regularly: the more you do this, the easier it gets. Over time, this can help you feel more at ease when you're with other people.

Remember, this exercise is about changing how you see social situations. It's a simple idea, but it can make a big difference to how you feel about yourself and others around you.

Going Solo

People may think it's strange or unusual to do things alone, like travelling or eating lunch at a restaurant. In truth, most people don't notice or mind if someone is doing something alone. The spotlight effect can undoubtedly make you feel otherwise. You might feel like everyone is watching you and thinking it's odd that you're alone, but this is just a trick your mind plays. People are usually too busy to pay much attention to what others are doing.

You need to remember a few things about going solo.

Most People Don't Notice: most people are focused on their own activities or thoughts, so they're not paying attention to whether others are alone.

It's OK to Be Alone: doing things alone can be a great experience. You can go at your own pace, do precisely what you want and enjoy some quiet time.

Facing the Fear: the more you do things alone, the easier it becomes. You start to realize that no one is judging you and you become more comfortable with it.

Benefits of Solo Activities: going solo can be really freeing. You learn more about yourself, become more independent and may even find it relaxing and enjoyable.

Making Hard Stuff Easy: The Going Solo Challenge

Goal: to embrace doing activities alone and overcome the fear of being judged for being on your own.

Duration: one full day

Morning: Preparation and Mindset

1. **Choose Your Activities:** start by planning two to three activities you usually wouldn't do alone. This could be having breakfast at a cafe, walking in a park, visiting a museum or watching a movie at a cinema.
2. **Set Your Intentions:** write down what you hope to gain from this challenge, whether feeling more independent, confident or comfortable in your own company.
3. **Mindfulness Moment:** take five to ten minutes to meditate or practise deep breathing, focusing on the excitement of new experiences rather than anxieties.

Throughout the Day: Solo Adventures

1. **Document Your Experience:** carry a notebook or use your phone to jot down how you feel before, during and after each activity. Note any anxious thoughts and how the actual experience compares to them.
2. **Stay Present:** during each activity, try to stay in the moment. Focus on your surroundings, the activity itself and the enjoyment of your own company.
3. **Challenge Negative Thoughts:** if you worry about being judged, remind yourself that most people are too focused on their own lives to notice others in detail.

Evening: Reflection and Growth

1. **Reflect on Your Day:** review your notes. Were there moments when you felt self-conscious? How did the reality compare to your expectations?
2. **Identify Learning Points:** what did you learn about yourself? Did you find certain activities more enjoyable than expected?
3. **Plan Your Next Solo Adventure:** based on today's experiences, consider other solo activities you might try. This could be something more challenging or a repeat of what you particularly enjoyed.

What It's All About

The Going Solo Challenge is about discovering the joys and freedoms of doing things yourself. It's a step towards breaking down the stigma of being alone in public places and growing more comfortable and confident in your own company. Remember, independence is a strength, and enjoying your own company is a form of self-care and empowerment.

Everyone is friendly, but everyone is scared of going first

It's important to remember that most people are friendly and would like to talk or be friends, but they are often too nervous to make the first move. It's like when you're at a party or a new class and want to start a conversation with someone. You might think they seem like a good person to be friends with, but you're worried about saying hello first. You're unsure if they will like you or want to talk. The thing is, the other person is probably feeling the same way. They might also think you seem friendly and want to chat, but they are scared to start talking first.

It's normal to feel shy or nervous about meeting new people. Still, it's also a reminder that if we take the first step, we might discover that the other person is happy we did. It's about being brave and starting the conversation, even when it feels scary. When someone goes first, it often leads to a good talk and maybe even a new friendship.

The Solo Day Plan

Plan your day of going solo using prompts from the section above. Reuse as needed and often.

Activities	
Intention	
Reflections	
Negative Points	
Learning Points	

Unshackle Your Thinking

Does it ever seem to you like your brain and your thoughts are playing a trick on you, making the problems or negative feelings seem much graver than they were in reality? It may not be far from true – but there is a solution that can help you put a stop to it. Cognitive restructuring is a technique used in CBT (cognitive behavioural therapy). It's about changing unhelpful or wrong ways of thinking. Often, people have what are called 'cognitive distortions'.

These ways of thinking twist things and give a bad or unhealthy view of what's happening.

It's critical to understand that all cognitive distortions:

1. are thinking habits or beliefs that we keep repeating
2. are thoughts that aren't true or are often overblown or exaggerated
3. show up as negative feelings or emotions
4. can lead to more worry and sadness and might even harm our mental health.

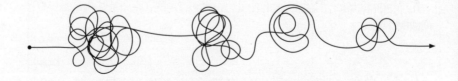

The Ten Cognitive Distortions

Below is a list of the ten cognitive distortions people experience daily. The better you understand and acknowledge them, the easier it is to identify the behaviour patterns and follow the four-step process to change them.

1. **All-or-Nothing Thinking:** seeing situations as just one of two extremes, like thinking something is either perfect or a total failure, instead of seeing the range of possibilities in between.

2. **Overgeneralization:** thinking that something that happened once or a few times will always happen.

3. **Mental Filtering:** paying attention only to the bad and not noticing the good parts.

4. **Disqualifying the Positive:** ignoring or thinking that good experiences or successes are unimportant.

5. **Jumping to Conclusions:** deciding something negative is true without any proof. This includes:

   - **Mind-Reading:** believing you know what others are thinking.
   - **Fortune-Telling:** predicting that things will go wrong even if they might not.

6. **Magnification (Catastrophizing) or Minimization:** making too much of something or making it seem less important than it really is.

7. **Emotional Reasoning:** believing that something must be true because you feel a certain way.

8. **'Should' and 'Must' Statements:** using 'should', 'must' or 'ought to' in a way that leads to disappointment or guilt. For

example, 'I should have known better' (this thought often occurs after an undesired outcome, leading to unnecessary guilt and self-blame) or 'I must do things perfectly' (this perfectionism can prevent us from starting tasks due to fear of not doing them perfectly, leading to procrastination and anxiety).

9. **Labelling and Mislabelling:** assigning negative labels to yourself or others based on things that have happened.

10. **Personalization:** believing you're to blame for things outside your control.

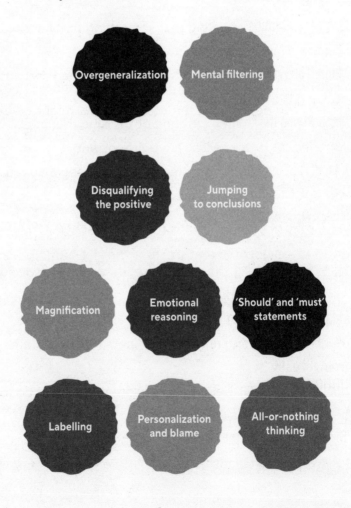

The Four Steps to Restructuring Cognitive Distortions

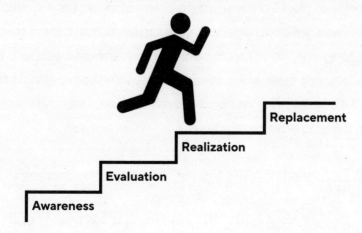

Awareness

The first step is to notice the thoughts automatically coming to your mind. You need to list the thoughts that might be causing problems. You must be aware of these thoughts before you try to change them. Don't judge or try to fix them yet.

For example, imagine you make a small mistake at work; instead of seeing it as a minor error, you start thinking it's a colossal disaster. You worry this small mistake will make your boss think you're not good at your job and that you might lose it. Notice every time you start thinking in this extreme way, called catastrophizing. Ask yourself, 'Is this really true?' If you're trying to guess what will happen in the future, you can be pretty sure it's not.

Evaluation

Next, it's time to start thinking more sensibly. After you've made a list of your thoughts, you can determine which thoughts are rational and which are not.

Why do you think making a mistake at work will cause you to lose your job? This fear might come from when you made a mistake and your manager was quite upset about it. Even though it was long ago, you can't forget how embarrassed you felt. This is why you get really anxious whenever you're completing a task, even if it's something you know how to do well. Thinking carefully about these questions can help you find an answer.

Realization

After we notice that a thought might be causing us trouble or isn't good for us, we can figure out why it's a problem. This is when we ask ourselves why we believe this thought, whether it's true and how true it is.

I can remind myself that it's OK to make mistakes because I'm only human. All I need to do is try my best. If I did lose my job because of a small mistake, it's not the end of the world. I could find another job – after all, I managed to get the job I have now.

Replacement

Lastly, think of other ways to see the situation that are more sensible. Our automatic thoughts often just happen without us realizing. So the goal isn't to stop these automatic thoughts but to notice when they are twisting reality and quickly think of something more sensible instead.

Change the thought *if I make a mistake, I'll be fired* to something more logical each time it comes up. You might instead say, 'I can't be sure if I don't make a mistake, I won't be fired, but I know

I've been here a long time and my last appraisal was excellent. And even if I lost this job, I could return to my old job.'

By changing the way you think, you can see things differently. The aim is to swap unrealistic thoughts with more down-to-earth ones, but this takes quite a bit of thinking and awareness of your own thoughts. For example:

Initial Thought: I've made a mistake. I'm going to get fired!
New Thought: I can't be sure that if I make a mistake, I won't be fired, but I know I've been here a long time and my last appraisal was excellent. And even if I lost this job, I could return to my old job.

By changing the way you think, you can see things differently. The aim is to swap unrealistic thoughts with more down-to-earth ones.

Making Hard Stuff Easy: Unshackle Your Thoughts

Goal: identify and understand the cognitive distortions in your daily thoughts and feelings.
Duration: one full day.

Morning: Setting the Stage

1. **Prepare Your Journal:** start your day by setting up a small notebook or digital document to jot down thoughts and feelings throughout the day.
2. **Brief Overview:** take a few minutes to read about common cognitive distortions (like all-or-nothing thinking, overgeneralization, mental filtering, etc.).

3. **Mindfulness Moment:** begin your day with a five-minute mindfulness exercise to centre yourself and set a conscious intention to observe your thoughts without judgement.

Throughout the Day: Observation and Notation

1. **Regular Check-Ins:** set an alarm or reminder every hour to pause and note down your thoughts and feelings. Be as honest and detailed as possible.
2. **Trigger Points:** pay special attention to moments of stress, decision-making, social interactions or other significant events. Write down how you feel and what you're thinking.
3. **Non-Judgemental Approach:** remember, the goal is observation, not correction or judgement. Just note your thoughts as they are.

Evening: Reflection and Analysis

1. **Review Your Notes:** at the end of your day, set aside some quiet time to review your journal.
2. **Identify the Distortions:** look for patterns in your thoughts and feelings that match common cognitive distortions. For example, did you engage in all-or-nothing thinking? Were you jumping to conclusions?
3. **Reflection Questions:** for each identified distortion, ask yourself:
   - Why did I think this way?
   - What triggered this thought?
   - How did it make me feel?
   - What could be a more balanced way of thinking about this?

4. **Summarize Your Insights:** write down your key learnings about how cognitive distortions appear in your daily life and how they affect your emotions and decisions.

Post-Challenge Action

1. **Plan Forward:** based on your insights, think of one or two ways you could address these distortions moving forward. This could be a daily affirmation, more mindfulness practice or even seeking professional guidance.
2. **Gratitude and Acknowledgement:** finally, express gratitude to yourself for taking this vital step towards self-awareness and mental well-being.

Remember, this challenge is about increasing your awareness and understanding of your own thought patterns. It's a crucial step towards positive mental health and well-being.

Notes

Principle 5

Don't Allow Feelings to Affect Your Future

The Wise Cactus

A wise old cactus stood in the heart of a vast desert. Despite the blistering sun and freezing nights, it remained solid and steady, a true survivor. One sunny morning, a battered fox approached the cactus. Its fur was messy and it looked scared out of its wits.

'Good day, little fox,' greeted the cactus warmly. 'Why do you look so scared?'

'I'm terrified of predators,' the fox confessed, trembling. 'I can't even go out to find food.'

With a kind voice, the cactus said, 'Fear can be tough, but it's part of life. Feeling scared is OK, but don't let it stop you from doing important things. You'll find you can do more than you think.'

Feeling braver, the fox thanked the cactus and moved away, its heart a little lighter.

That same evening, a lonely coyote with a sad, distant look in its eyes wandered near the cactus. It seemed lost and unsure.

'What's on your mind, coyote?' the cactus enquired.

'I feel so alone,' the coyote shared. 'I'm scared to meet others. What if they don't like me?'

Standing tall under the stars, the cactus advised, 'Sometimes, we need others to truly shine, like stars in the night. Being brave means facing those fears. Give your pack a chance. They might welcome you more warmly than you expect.'

With a new sense of hope, the coyote gave a small smile and headed off to find its pack.

The next day, a scorpion came along, its tail raised high and full of anger.

'What's making you so angry, scorpion?' the cactus asked calmly, not intimidated by its hostility.

'I'm angry at everyone! I want to sting them, so they know how I feel,' the scorpion said bitterly. 'Maybe then they'll understand and be nicer to me.'

The cactus responded gently. 'Anger can cloud your thoughts. It's like trying to see your reflection in boiling water. Find peace within yourself first and you'll find it easier to get along with others.'

After a moment of thought, the scorpion's anger seemed to fade and it decided to seek understanding instead of revenge.

As the sun set on the third day, the cactus remained in the harsh desert, looking proudly at the fox, the coyote and the scorpion, their silhouettes becoming smaller and smaller on the horizon as they set off into the world to seek new adventures, no longer bound by anxieties or rage.

The story of The Wise Cactus teaches us three important lessons through the cactus's meetings with a scared fox, a lonely coyote and an angry scorpion.

First, we learn not to let fear stop us from doing important things in life. The fox realizes that feeling afraid is OK, but it shouldn't prevent it from going out to find food.

Second, the story shows us how valuable having connections with others is. The coyote understands that sometimes we need to be brave and give others a chance to avoid feeling alone.

Finally, the tale cautions against letting anger control us. The scorpion learns that finding inner calm is better than lashing out in anger at others.

Through kind advice, the wise cactus helps these desert animals overcome their worries of fear, loneliness and anger. It inspires them to live life fully, make friends and find peace within themselves.

Weathering the Storm

'Weathering the storm' means that we're managing to get through a challenging situation without too much harm or damage. It's fascinating to compare our feelings to the weather because there are many similarities.

Impermanence

Just as the weather is constantly changing, so are our feelings. A sunny day might suddenly turn stormy, much like how a happy moment can quickly shift to sadness or worry. Realizing that our emotions are constantly moving and aren't fixed can be freeing. It helps us experience these feelings without becoming too overwhelmed or letting them dictate our actions.

Imagine a clear blue sky suddenly filling with clouds. That's like a calm mind becoming clouded by worry. But just as clouds eventually pass so do these anxious thoughts. Or think of a gentle drizzle that slowly turns into a downpour; it's like how a minor annoyance can grow into real anger. Yet even the heaviest rain stops in time and anger fades away.

By seeing our emotions as weather patterns that come and go, we learn not to fear them. We understand they're just part of life, not something that has to control us. This way, we can feel better prepared for life's ups and downs, knowing that no feeling lasts forever.

Unpredictable Nature

The weather is often full of surprises. Despite advanced technology, nature has a way of catching us off guard. Our emotions are much the same – we don't always know how we're going to feel next. Sometimes, we feel happy, sad or worried without reason. This shows just how complicated our thoughts and emotions can be.

Just as a sunny day suddenly turns rainy, our mood can change without warning. You might wake up cheerful but something minor happens and your mood shifts. It's like when a sudden gust of wind blows away the clouds and suddenly it's sunny again. Our feelings can change just as quickly.

This unpredictability of emotions, like the weather, reminds us that it's OK not to have everything under control. Just as we carry an umbrella for unexpected rain, we can prepare ourselves to handle sudden changes in our mood. Understanding that our emotions, like the weather, are beyond our control helps us be more patient and kinder to ourselves.

External vs Internal Conditions

The weather happens outside and changes the world around us. In the same way, things that happen in our lives can affect how we feel. But just like protecting ourselves from bad weather, we can also learn to deal with our emotions, no matter what's happening around us.

Think about how we wear a coat to stay warm in cold weather or find a safe place when it's stormy. Similarly, we can find ways to comfort ourselves when we are upset or stressed. This might mean talking to a friend when we're feeling down or taking a few deep breaths to calm ourselves when we're anxious.

Just as we check the weather forecast to prepare for the day, we can also become more aware of our feelings. We can better handle these emotions by understanding what makes us happy, sad or angry. It's like learning to carry an umbrella in case it rains – we can prepare ourselves for difficult times.

This way, we realize that even though we can't control everything around us, we can control how we respond. We learn that, like the weather, our surroundings might affect us, but they don't have to decide how we feel inside.

Necessity for Preparation

Farmers plan for different seasons, sailors study the tides and we look at the weather forecast before leaving home. Similarly, by knowing our emotional patterns, we can be more prepared to deal with the changes in our feelings.

Just as a farmer prepares the fields for planting or harvest depending on the season, we can prepare for different emotional states. For example, if certain situations make us anxious, we can learn techniques to calm ourselves down, like deep breathing or talking to a friend.

Sailors use their knowledge of the tides to navigate the seas safely. Likewise understanding what makes us happy or sad can steer us through tough times. It's like having a map for our emotions, which helps us to find our way when things get complicated.

Checking the weather forecast is something we do to decide if we need an umbrella or a sun hat. Understanding our emotions works in much the same way. If we know we're going through a tough time, we can prepare ourselves, just like we would dress appropriately for bad weather.

By being aware of our emotional patterns, we're better equipped to handle the ups and downs of our feelings. This doesn't mean we won't ever feel sad or upset, but we'll be better prepared to deal with these feelings when they come.

The Beauty in All Conditions

Every type of weather, be it a gentle rain or a powerful storm, holds its own beauty and reason for being. Similarly, every emotion we experience – happiness, sadness, anger or love – brings depth and variety to our lives. Rather than thinking of some emotions as bad, we can start to see them as valuable parts of our life's journey.

Think about how rain helps plants to grow and how a storm can clear the air. These weather conditions, though sometimes inconvenient, have essential roles in nature. In the same way, our emotions, even the difficult ones, have a purpose. They help us understand ourselves and the world better.

Just as a landscape looks more interesting with a mix of sunshine and clouds, our lives become more prosperous and packed with different feelings. Happiness brings joy and energy, while sadness can help us appreciate the good times more. Even anger has its place, perhaps showing us that something needs to change.

When we start to see the beauty in all kinds of weather, we can enjoy being outside no matter what the sky looks like. And when we begin to appreciate all our emotions, we can live more fully, experiencing each feeling as part of the beautiful tapestry of life. This way, we learn not just to endure each emotion but to find its value and beauty, understanding that each one has something to teach us.

Your Feelings vs Your Future

Understanding your feelings is crucial to living a full life, as they shape how we see everything around us. Feelings let us know what's happening inside and are our body's way of telling us about our experiences.

Our feelings allow us to go through many different emotions. They enable us to feel life's happiness and sadness and all its highs and lows. They're also crucial in building relationships, making big decisions and understanding how we respond to different situations.

However, we often struggle with how we react to our feelings. It's important to realize that emotional reactions come from mental habits. Our emotions aren't just about what's happening now. They're triggered by how our brain interprets events through the lens of our past experiences. This emotional reaction is something we learn, which means we can also learn new ways to think and react if we choose to.

My feelings framework is designed to help you recognize and understand your feelings. It encourages you to notice how you react to these feelings and to consciously work on acknowledging and improving them.

The Feelings Framework (REACT)

The REACT framework is a comprehensive approach to understanding and managing emotions designed to enhance emotional intelligence and well-being.

R = Recognize the Emotion: identifying and acknowledging your emotions. Pausing, reflecting and being honest with yourself about what you're feeling and why.

E = Explore the Origin: tracing back to the start of your feelings to recognize patterns and gain insight into how your past experiences, current environment and physical states influence your emotional reactions.

A = Accept Without Judgement: embracing your emotions without labelling them as good or bad and understanding that emotions are transient.

C = Communicate or Channel: learning to express your emotions in healthy ways. Engaging in creative activities, practising mindfulness and channelling emotions into constructive action.

T = Transform Perspective: challenging negative thought patterns, seeking alternative viewpoints and finding positive things to be grateful for.

R = Recognize the Emotion

Before dealing with any emotion, you must recognize and accept that you're feeling it. This means you must listen to yourself and understand what you're feeling right now. Here's how you can do it:

Stop and reflect. Take a moment to pause whatever you're doing. This helps you focus on what's going on inside you.

Ask yourself questions like, 'How am I feeling right now?' or 'What's making me feel this way?'. This helps you pinpoint your emotions.

Be honest with yourself. It's OK to feel whatever you feel. Don't try to hide it or pretend it's not there.

Notice physical signs. Sometimes, our bodies show our emotions before we're fully aware of them. You might feel a knot in your stomach when you're anxious or your heart might race when you're scared.

Doing this helps you get in touch with your emotions. It's like learning to read a map of your feelings. Once you know where you are on the map, figuring out where to go next is much easier.

The Emotion Wheel

A helpful tool to figure out your feelings is the emotion wheel. This wheel can be an excellent place to start to work out why you feel the way you do, what your feelings are trying to show you and what you can do about it. Understanding your emotions is the first step in getting to know your feelings better.

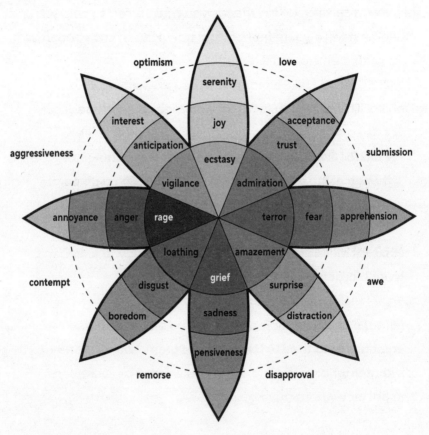

E= Explore the Origin

Understanding the root of your emotions is vital. If you can figure out what sparked it, you're in a much better position to tackle the feeling right at its source. Here's how to go about it:

Trace the emotion's beginning: remember when you first noticed this emotion. What were you doing? Who were you with? Sometimes, the starting point of an emotion is not apparent, but if you think carefully, you might find a clue.

Look for patterns: do you often feel this way in similar situations or with certain people? Recognizing patterns can help you understand if your emotion is linked to specific events, environments or individuals.

Consider external influences: external factors like stress, lack of sleep or weather can affect our emotions. Think about what's been happening in your life that might influence your feelings.

Reflect on personal history: sometimes, our emotions are connected to our past experiences. A current situation might remind you, even subconsciously, of something from your past, triggering a particular feeling.

By exploring these aspects, you start unravelling the mystery of your emotions. The more you know why you feel a certain way, the better you can manage your emotional responses.

A = Accept Without Judgement

Rather than pushing your emotions away or feeling bad about having them, it is essential to accept them as a regular part of being human. This doesn't mean you agree with any negative things you might do because of these feelings. It just means you

recognize and accept the emotion without being hard on yourself.
Here are some steps to help assist you:

Practise self-kindness: tell yourself that it's completely normal
and OK to have emotions. Everyone has them and they're a
natural part of life.

Don't label emotions as good or bad: try to see your emotions as
neither good nor bad. They're just feelings and every feeling
has a purpose or message.

Remember that feelings change: keep in mind that emotions
aren't permanent. They come and go, and how you feel right
now might not be how you feel in a little while.

Reflect on what the emotion teaches: every emotion can teach
you something about yourself, others or a situation. Try to
see what you can learn from what you're feeling.

Avoid self-criticism: don't be hard on yourself when you notice
an emotion. Instead, acknowledge it as a natural response to
a situation or thought.

Following these steps teaches you to be more understanding and patient with yourself. Accepting your emotions without
judgement is vital to managing them effectively and growing
emotionally. It's about understanding yourself better and treating yourself with the same kindness and patience you would offer
to a good friend.

C = Communicate or Channel

Finding effective and positive ways to express what you're feeling is really important. When you do this, you can prevent your emotions from becoming too intense or hard to handle. It's like the steam coming from a kettle – it stops things from boiling over. Expressing your emotions can also help you get a clearer picture of your feelings and why. Here are some steps to help:

Talk to someone: if you're OK with it, share your feelings with a friend or family member. Talking can help you feel less alone and more understood.

Find creative outlets: activities like writing in a diary, creating art or doing some form of physical exercise can be great ways to process and understand your emotions. These activities allow you to express yourself safely and constructively.

Mindfulness: if your emotions feel too much, grounding techniques (like focusing on your senses or breathing) or practising mindfulness (being fully present in the moment) can help calm your mind.

Channel emotions into action: sometimes, positive action can help channel your emotions. For example, if you're feeling frustrated about something, see if there's a constructive way to address the situation.

Write it down: if you're not ready to talk to someone, writing down your thoughts and feelings can be an excellent first step. It helps clear your mind and might make it easier to talk about them later.

By following these steps, you create a safe space for your emotions. This not only helps in managing them but also in understanding yourself better. Remember, healthily expressing emotions is a vital part of your emotional well-being.

T = Transform Perspective

Changing how you look at a situation or emotion can really help. This means turning negative or unhelpful thinking into more positive or neutral thinking. It's like looking at a picture from a different angle – you might see something you didn't notice before. Here are some steps to help:

Spot negative thinking: first, try to notice if you have any negative or unhelpful thoughts linked to how you're feeling. These might be things like 'I always mess up' or 'Nothing ever goes right for me'.

Question these thoughts: ask yourself if these thoughts are really true. Is there evidence that shows a different story? Maybe you don't always mess up – think of times when you've done well.

Look for different viewpoints: try to see the situation from another angle. If a friend were in your shoes, what would you tell them? This can help you be fairer and kinder to yourself.

Find things to be thankful for: there might be something good even in tough times. Focusing on small things you're grateful for can help change your mood and outlook.

Look for the positives: even if it's small, try to find a positive aspect or a lesson you can learn from the situation. This helps shift your focus from what's going wrong to what might be going right or what you can learn.

You're training your mind to think more rationally and positively. This doesn't mean ignoring the bad things, just not letting them control how you see everything. Changing your perspective can significantly impact how you feel and respond to life's challenges.

Making Hard Stuff Easy: The Emotion Deep Dive

Objective: to understand the origins of your emotions in a simple one-day activity.

Steps for the Day

1. **Morning reflection:** start your day by thinking about how you're feeling. Are you happy, sad, anxious or calm? Write down your primary emotion.
2. **Midday check-in:** around lunchtime, take a moment to note your current emotions. What are you feeling now? Write it down, along with what you're doing and who you're with.
3. **Evening review:** in the evening, reflect on your emotions throughout the day. Write down any strong feelings you

experienced. Think about what might have caused these emotions. Were you stressed, tired or reacting to something someone said?

4. **Look for a pattern:** look at your notes at the end of the day. Do you see any patterns? For example, do you always feel a certain way at work or around certain people?

5. **Connect to past experiences:** consider whether any of today's emotions remind you of past experiences. Does a current situation bring back old feelings?

This exercise will help you become more aware of your emotions and their triggers. By tracking your feelings throughout the day and reflecting on their possible origins, you can start to understand your emotional patterns.

Notes

Principle 6

Be Present

The King and the Pauper

In a kingdom where the hustle of daily life never ceased, a king was overwhelmed by his royal duties. His days, from the first light of dawn to the last glimmer of dusk, were crammed with endless meetings, difficult decisions and a mountain of documents demanding his signature. Despite living in a palace adorned with gold and finery, emptiness echoed in his heart. Gazing at his sprawling kingdom, he often murmured, 'There must be more to life than this . . .'

Curious whispers about a pauper living on the fringes of the kingdom reached the king's ears. This pauper, despite his meagre means, was known for his infectious laughter and boundless joy. Confused, and eager to understand the source of such happiness, the king donned a disguise one night and slipped away from the palace.

He found the pauper in a humble abode, which was small yet filled with warmth and welcome. This stark contrast to his own grand but hollow palace puzzled the king. Looking around with wonder and disbelief, the king asked, 'How do you find joy in such simplicity? I have every luxury in my palace, yet they feel lifeless.'

The pauper hesitated for a second and then responded with a gentle, knowing smile. 'True joy, my lord, isn't housed in grand walls or crafted from gold. I learned this the hard way. When I had everything, I felt nothing.'

The pauper revealed his past as they shared a simple meal by the light of a single candle. He had once aspired for greatness, chasing dreams far beyond his grasp, neglecting the natural treasures in life. 'In my blind pursuit, I pushed away the ones I loved most,' he said, his voice tinged with regret. 'My family left me and I spiralled into hardship. It was in those darkest moments that I found clarity. The joy in a sunrise, children's laughter, the peace of gazing at the stars – these simple pleasures hold the true essence of happiness.'

The king visited the pauper frequently, each time leaving the palace's confines to learn more from this man of simple means. Together, they roamed the countryside, helping those in need and discovering the beauty of nature. The king started to see the world through new eyes and learned to appreciate the moment, whether in the chaos of court life or the quiet of a starlit night.

One day, the king let out a deep sigh of regret. 'I fear I've led my kingdom astray in my quest for more. I've been blind to the heart of my people.'

The pauper shook his head. 'Acknowledging this is your first step towards change. It's never too late to find the real treasures in life.'

When the king returned to his palace, he initiated reforms to alleviate his people's suffering. But the most profound change came one night, under a canopy of stars, as he sat again with the pauper.

The pauper began to recount part of his life previously untold. 'I once served in your royal court,' he revealed, 'toiling into the night on projects designed to enhance the palace's glory.'

The king listened, his discomfort growing.

'I worked tirelessly, but it was never enough. My family at home suffered due to my absence and stress. Eventually, it all fell apart.' The pauper's voice cracked with emotion. 'I lost my family, then my home.'

Realizing his own demands had played a role in the pauper's downfall, the king felt profound guilt. His luxurious pursuits now seemed utterly meaningless. From that moment, he vowed to rule with a new perspective that prioritized his people over grandeur.

The story of the king and the pauper became a tale told in every household of the kingdom, reminding us that the best things in life are often the simplest and how important it is to enjoy the here and now and to be brave enough to change so we don't lose what's truly important to us.

Why We Struggle to Be Present

The Way Our Brains Are Wired

Think of your brain as an old-fashioned warning system constantly looking for potential danger. In the distant past, safety often meant being vigilant for threats such as wild animals or unexpected risks. We relied on our brains to remember past dangers (like recalling a dangerous animal hiding in a bush) and to anticipate future challenges (such as wondering whether a gathering storm would turn severe).

Fast-forward to modern-day life. Although our daily lives don't involve evading wild animals on our way to the supermarket, our brains are still programmed to be cautious and alert to potential problems. This means we often find ourselves preoccupied with thoughts about future events, fretting about what might happen tomorrow, next week or even years ahead. We spend so much time ruminating over past events, replaying scenarios and asking, 'What if I had acted differently?'

This age-old alert system in our brains makes it challenging to live in the present. Physically, we might be in one place. Still, our minds can frequently be elsewhere – either wandering back to the

'You can't change the past, but you can ruin the present by worrying about the future'

– Isak Dinesen

past or straying into the future. As a result, genuinely enjoying the present moment becomes a tricky task.

This constant back-and-forth between the past and the future can become mentally exhausting. It's as if our brains are running a never-ending marathon, with thoughts racing from one time zone to another. This can lead to feelings of anxiety, stress or even sadness as we struggle to focus on the here and now.

Life is like a Theme Park

Imagine you're at a theme park. There are bright lights everywhere, lots of different music and loud announcements, and the smells of hot dogs and sweets are all around. You see people everywhere, queuing up for the latest white-knuckle ride or running to the next live show before it closes its doors. It's fun but also a bit too much for your senses, isn't it? Think about your everyday life as being constantly at this theme park.

In the world today, your phone is like a small theme park in your pocket. It keeps lighting up with messages, making noises and vibrating from texts, emails and apps. Each one seems to be saying, 'Look here!' Your TV or computer adds more noise with news that's on all day and night. Even when you're not looking at screens, you see adverts on boards, buses and hear them whenever you switch on the radio. All these things are like the rides and games at the theme park, always trying to get your attention. With so much happening, it's hard to just stop and enjoy one thing, like having a quiet chat with a friend or eating lunch without looking at your phone.

This never-ending stream of things can make it hard to be in the moment. Your brain gets used to jumping from one thing to another, so staying focused on what's happening now can feel as tricky as ignoring someone juggling with fire right next to you. Also, being constantly switched on like this can make you feel tired. Just as a day at a theme park can leave you worn out, the constant buzz of life today can make you feel mentally exhausted.

Living in today's world with all its distractions is like trying to find a quiet place in a busy, loud theme park. You must try to escape the noise, turn off the constant stream of things grabbing your attention and find quiet times in your day. Just like you might look for a calm spot to sit and rest at the theme park, we all need to find ways to switch off and relax in our everyday lives, enjoying the peace of being there in the moment.

Mastering Presence. Yes, again

Imagine going back to when you learned how to ride a bike. It was tough at first. As you pedalled, you wobbled, tumbled and needed someone to steady the bike. Being fully in the moment, or present, is similar. We're not naturally good at it; we must learn it and practise it.

Just as you learn to balance on a bike, you must learn to stop your mind from drifting to the past or future. Mindfulness is like stabilizers for this. It helps you practise staying calm and focused on the here and now. Mindfulness can be as easy as focusing on your breathing, noticing things around you or simply feeling the floor beneath your feet. But if no one has ever taught you how to do this – if you've never been trained – it's like trying to ride a bike for the first time without help. You might be unsure what to do and end up stuck. That's why it's helpful to learn and practise ways to keep your mind in the present (mindfulness exercises). They teach your brain to ignore distractions and let you enjoy being in the present moment.

Here are three presence practices you can use throughout the day:

Pause and Notice

Several times throughout your day, just pause and notice what's happening in your environment and within you. This could be done anytime, like before starting a new task or even in the middle of one.

The Three-Minute Breathing Space

This quick exercise is useful when you feel overwhelmed. Spend one minute simply noticing your experience, including thoughts, feelings and physical sensations. Spend the second minute focusing on your breath. Expand your attention back to your whole body and the environment around you on the last minute.

The Body-Scan Meditation

Lie down or sit comfortably. Focus your attention slowly and deliberately on each part of your body, from your toes to your head. As you focus on each part, notice any sensations, tension or discomfort. Breathe into these sensations, imagining tension leaving your body with each exhale.

Becoming a Professional Plate Spinner

Our lives are like trying to keep lots of plates spinning at once. We're always busy trying to keep each plate going. We can't focus on just one because we're too busy moving between them all.

We might answer an email while listening to a podcast and watching the kids. Or we could be working on something, but then we stop to look at our phone or have a chat. People often say doing lots of things at once is good – it's meant to show we're efficient and busy. But here's the thing: our brains aren't made to do so many things at the same time. When we try to do too much, we can't give our best to anything. It's like being OK at many things but not exceptional at anything. We only provide a little attention to each task, so it's easier to make mistakes and might take longer to finish them. We end up with lots of half-done tasks – like the plates, we just can't keep them all going perfectly. Instead of enjoying what we do, we rush through it, and the quality of our work – and how much we enjoy it – can suffer.

So how can we get better at plate spinning? Here are some tips:

1 **Choose your plates wisely:** not every plate is equally important. Some, like family, friends and loved ones, need more of our attention. Other plates don't need as much time and effort, and even if they wobble and fall, they usually bounce instead of break, meaning you can pick them up and start again later.
2 **Get help with some plates:** it's easier to spin plates with a bit of help. Sort your plates into those only you can do and those others can help with, then find people to help you with those.
3 **Don't take on too many plates:** the most powerful word in the English language is 'no'. You have too many plates because you keep adding others' plates to yours. Get better at focusing on your own plates and say no to any more.

4   **It takes energy and focus to spin plates:** spinning plates is hard when you're tired. Make sure you take time to recharge, rest and recover.

FOMO (Fear of Missing Out)

Imagine you're at home, reading a book or just trying to chill, but your phone is nearby. Every now and then, you hear a text coming through, or maybe it's just sitting there quietly but you're aware it's your link to all your mates and the internet. You can't shake this nagging feeling that you might be missing out on something.

When was the last time you experienced FOMO?

This feeling is known as fear of missing out or FOMO. It's like you're quietly sitting in a garden, enjoying the calm, but you can't shake off the thought that there's a loud, fun party happening in the house next door that you're missing out on. This makes it really tough to enjoy the quiet, your book or just relax because part of you is always wondering about the 'what ifs'.

Often you might find yourself grabbing your phone, flicking through social media, looking at photos and stories, and trying to catch up with what everyone else is doing. That's FOMO at work – a constant worry that pulls your mind away from the peaceful garden where you are, making you think about parties or gatherings you're not part of. It's tough to shake off this feeling because we're naturally inclined to want to be part of the group, to be in the know and not feel left out. It takes a real effort to put your phone down, resist that temptation and focus on enjoying what you're doing right at that moment.

Making Hard Stuff Easy: Six Tips for Being More Present

#1 JOMO (Joy of Missing Out)

JOMO, or the joy of missing out, is the happy opposite of FOMO. It's all about finding pleasure in not being part of everything and enjoying your own company or the smaller, quieter moments. When you start feeling the pull of FOMO, think about JOMO instead. It's like being content in your cosy room while there's a noisy party next door. You're at peace with staying in, maybe reading a book, watching your favourite TV show or just having a cup of tea. JOMO is about realizing that sometimes the best place to be is exactly where you are, doing what makes you feel relaxed and happy, away from the hustle and bustle.

#2 The Art of Single-Tasking

The idea behind single-tasking is simple: do one thing at a time and give it your full attention. When you're eating, for instance, just focus on your meal. Enjoy every bite, taste the different flavours and don't get distracted by the TV or scrolling through your phone. The same goes for when you're walking. Instead of being on your phone or lost in your thoughts about other things, just concentrate on your walk. Pay attention to the rhythm of your steps, the feel of the ground under your feet, the fresh air and the sights and sounds around you.

Single-tasking teaches your brain to focus on the task at hand. It's about training your mind to avoid getting side-tracked by trying to do too many things at once. Often, we think that by multitasking, we're being more efficient. This can lead to a cluttered mind and less effective work. When you single-task, you'll probably find that you do things better and enjoy them more because you're fully engaged. For example, if you're gardening, just focus on that. Feel the soil in your hands, notice the colours of the flowers and enjoy the peacefulness of being outside. Or if you're writing a letter or an email, concentrate solely on expressing your thoughts clearly without the distraction of background noise or other tasks.

By practising single-tasking, you can also find it easier to relax and reduce stress. It helps you slow down and appreciate the moment, whether that's having a cup of tea, listening to music or chatting with a friend. You might notice details and pleasures you've missed before when your attention was split between multiple things. Savour the moment and find joy in the simple tasks of everyday life.

#3 Digital Detox

Plan to set aside specific times in your day or week when you switch off your digital devices like your phone, tablet and computer. Turn them off completely or put them away so you won't be tempted to check them. This break from endless notifications and alerts allows you to step back from the online world.

You'll find more time to engage with the natural world when you're not constantly checking your devices. You might notice things you've missed, like having a face-to-face conversation with someone, reading a book or simply enjoying the peace and quiet. It also helps you appreciate life's simple things, like going for a walk, cooking a meal or spending time with family and friends without distractions.

A digital detox can also reduce the feeling of FOMO that often comes from seeing what others are doing on social media. It's easy to feel like you're missing out on something when being bombarded with updates and photos from others.

This digital detox isn't about completely cutting technology out of your life – it's about finding a healthier balance. Start with just an hour a day or perhaps a whole day over the weekend. During this time, engage in activities that you enjoy or that relax you, and pay attention to how you feel during and after this detox period. Many people feel calmer, more focused and more content when taking regular breaks from their digital devices.

#4 Nature Time

Make sure to spend some time out in nature. This could be anything from a short walk in a local park to a day in the country-side or by the sea. Nature has its own slow and steady rhythm, which is very different from the fast-paced world we're used to. Being surrounded by trees, plants and wildlife or simply breathing in fresh air can calm your mind.

Try to really notice your surroundings. Listen to the sounds – maybe the rustling of leaves, birds chirping or a stream's gentle flow. Look at the shades of green in the trees and plants, how the light plays on the water or how the clouds move across the sky. Feel the ground under your feet as you walk, the warmth of the sun or the breeze on your face.

Spending time in nature helps to slow down your racing thoughts. This can be especially helpful if you're feeling stressed or overwhelmed. It's a chance to escape your daily worries and be present in the natural world.

So try to include some nature time in your routine, even if it's just a short while each day. It's a simple but effective way to relax and recharge, and it's also good for your mental and physical health.

#5 Attentive Listening

When you're having a conversation with someone, make an effort to listen with your full attention. This means focusing on what the other person is saying, not just hearing the words but understanding their feelings and thoughts. Try not to think about what you'll say next or get distracted by what's happening around you or in your mind.

This isn't just about being polite; it makes a big difference to your relationships. When people feel genuinely heard, it strengthens your connection with them. They're more likely to trust and respect you, and you'll probably find they're more willing to listen to you in return. This helps build stronger, more meaningful relationships with friends, family or colleagues.

Paying close attention when someone else is speaking helps you stay anchored in the present moment. Instead of your mind wandering off to something that happened earlier or worrying about the future, you're focused on what's happening right now.

When you're listening, you might pick up on things you'd otherwise miss – subtle tones in their voice that show how they're feeling or details in their story that give you a deeper understanding of their perspective. This can lead to more exciting and rewarding conversations and a greater sense of empathy and understanding.

So, next time you're talking to someone, try to put aside other distractions and give them your complete attention. Notice how this changes the conversation and how it makes you feel. You might be surprised at how much more connected and present you feel just by listening attentively.

#6 Practising Mindfulness

Set aside a little bit of time every day to practise mindfulness. Mindfulness is about paying attention to what's happening now – what you're feeling, thinking and sensing. It's a skill that helps you become more aware of when your mind starts to drift off into other thoughts and it teaches you how to gently steer it back to the present. This can be done by using apps that guide you in mindfulness or joining a class.

You don't need much time for this – just a few minutes daily can make a big difference. You can try doing it in a quiet place where you won't be disturbed. Sit comfortably, close your eyes if you like and start by focusing on your breathing. Notice how the air feels as it enters and leaves your nose or mouth, and how your chest rises and falls. If your mind wanders – for example, towards what you need to do later – that's OK. It's part of the process.

The important thing is to notice that your mind has wandered and gently bring your focus back to your breathing.

As you keep practising, you'll likely find it easier to stay present without worrying about the past or future. It can help you feel more relaxed and peaceful, improve your concentration and make you more aware of the little joys in life. Remember, it's not about perfecting it; it's about being kind to yourself and giving your mind a break from the busy world.

Making Hard Stuff Easy: Staying Present

This one-day challenge will enhance your ability to be present and mindful throughout the day and get you to truly understand what mindfulness is all about.

Morning (7–9 a.m.)

Mindful Breathing (5 minutes): start your day with a five-minute mindful breathing exercise. Sit in a quiet place, close your eyes and focus solely on your breathing. Notice the rise and fall of your chest and your breath's sound and rhythm.

Mindful Breakfast: eat your breakfast without distractions like your phone or TV. Pay attention to the taste, texture and smell of your food. Chew slowly and appreciate each bite.

Mid-Morning (11 a.m.)

Mindful Eating: as at breakfast, if you're having a mid-morning snack, eat it more mindfully. Focus on the flavours and sensations of eating rather than eating mechanically while doing something else.

Afternoon (3 p.m.)

Mindfulness Tea/Coffee Break: brew a cup of tea or coffee. Focus on the process of making it, the aroma, the warmth of the cup in your hands and the taste.

Evening (6-8 p.m.)

Mindful Cooking and Dinner: while cooking, pay attention to the colours of the ingredients, the sounds of cooking and the aromas. Eat your dinner mindfully, as you did with breakfast and lunch.

Mindful Reflection (5 minutes): reflect on your day. Think about the moments you felt most present. Acknowledge these moments without judgement.

Before Bed (9–11 p.m.)

Mindful Relaxation (5 minutes): engage in a relaxation technique, like a body-scan meditation or breathing exercise, focusing on the sensations in each part of your body.

Mindful Journalling (5 minutes): write down your experience of the day. Note any challenges you faced in staying mindful and how you felt during different parts of the challenge.

Tips for Success

- Keep your phone and other distractions away during mindful activities.
- If your mind wanders, gently bring it back to the present task.

- Remember, the goal is not to perfect mindfulness but to experience the process of being present.

Notes

Principle 7

Hard Stuff, Easy Life; Easy Stuff, Hard Life

The Lost Oasis

In the vast open savannah was a large, sun-baked lakebed that had been dry for years. The animals in the area had given up on it, making long, tiring journeys to find water in distant places. But there was one elderly elephant who still remembered the lake as it once had been, brimming with water and teeming with life. The image of the oasis this place had once been kept coming back to it. Seeing the lake so empty and lifeless now filled it with sadness.

Never losing hope, the elephant began digging into the lakebed's hard cracked earth. It used its mighty tusks and large, strong feet, determined to find water. The other animals watched, some with curiosity, others with disbelief. 'Why bother with that old lake?' they muttered to the elephant. But the elephant paid them no attention and kept digging daily.

Then, one sunny morning, something remarkable happened. As the elephant dug, water suddenly started to gush out from beneath the ground, transforming the dry, dusty landscape into a lively, bustling waterhole.

The change was astonishing. The once barren land around the lake sprang back to life. Green shoots pushed through the earth, trees began to flourish and flowers bloomed in bright splashes of colour. The news of the reawakened lake spread quickly, and animals from all over the savannah came to see this miracle.

They found the old elephant standing proudly by the water's edge, its eyes twinkling joyfully. The once sceptical animals now looked at the elephant with admiration and respect. 'You've shown us that a little patience and hard work can make dreams come true,' they said, bowing their heads in gratitude.

The elephant's story became a legend on the savannah. It was a tale told to inspire perseverance. It reminded everyone that even in the face of doubt and adversity, a determined heart could bring about true wonders.

Why People Struggle to Do the Hard Stuff

If you find it hard to do demanding tasks, congratulations, you're human with a perfectly normal brain. Our brains are wired to keep us safe. This means they often alert us to potential dangers and activities that use a lot of energy. When something is difficult, it usually triggers a fear and stress response in our brains, setting off a fight or flight reaction. This reaction is beneficial when we're in danger but not so much when faced with a tricky task that needs concentration and calmness.

Now let's talk about energy. The brain uses a significant amount of energy – it accounts for about 20 per cent of the body's energy use, even though it's only 2 per cent of its weight. In simpler terms, that's around 0.3 kilowatt-hours (kWh) per day for an average adult, over a hundred times more than what a typical smartphone uses.

In the past, when food (our primary energy source) wasn't always easy to find, our brains evolved to save energy whenever possible. This is another reason we might find it hard to start or continue challenging tasks. Our brains try to be efficient by avoiding high-energy activities unless necessary.

Like training a muscle, the more you use it, the stronger and more efficient it becomes. So, the next time you're struggling with a challenging task, remember it's not just a lack of willpower – it's your brain doing what it's evolved to do. Understanding this can help us be kinder to ourselves and find better ways to stay disciplined and push through the challenges.

Five Things Stopping You from Doing the Hard Stuff

#1 Procrastination

Have you ever had something big and vital to do but found yourself reorganizing your sock drawer or putting all the spices in your spice rack alphabetically?

Congratulations, you've experienced procrastination.

When we have a task that needs a lot of thinking, we switch to doing something less important or even something that's not important at all. This habit of putting things off can come from different fears and ways of thinking. I've listed the three most important ones and how to improve and change them.

The Fear of Failure

Many procrastinate because they fear they won't meet others' expectations or successfully finish a challenging task. This fear can be overwhelming, stopping us from even starting the task. When there's a chance of not succeeding, the worry about failing can be stronger than our logical understanding of how significant or urgent the task is. Our brains try to stop or protect us from finishing the task.

You Can't Fail If You Don't Give Up

When I talk about doing hard things, it's usually about doing them consistently. It's not just about doing a hard thing once; it's about doing these things every day. I've been posting on social media daily for over a decade. About a year ago, I posted something that got very few views. Someone commented, *Dude, your account is dead; just give up.* I replied, *You can't fail if you don't give up.*

Three months after that post, I got some of the highest views on my content and grew my audience by over 500,000 on the platform. If I had given up, I would have failed. But the real key to content creation is showing up consistently and posting. Some posts might get a few views and others might go viral. The important thing is not to be put off by the results but to keep up the habit of posting.

Success in anything isn't about one big effort but lots of small efforts done consistently over time. I like to use the analogy of 'One Chapter Per Day'. If I gave you thirty-four books that could change your life, you might start the year reading three to four books. You might read a couple more in February and maybe finish another in March. But as time passes, it gets harder to start a new book, let alone finish it, and you might end the year having read only six out of thirty-four books. That's the fear of failure, making it harder to get going.

My 'One Chapter Per Day' approach doesn't focus on the total number of books. It's about the habit of reading a chapter every day. This task usually takes about twenty minutes and fits most people's busy schedules. If you read one chapter a day, you'll likely finish all thirty-four books I recommend. Small, consistent steps lead to significant achievements over time, and it's a great way to tackle big tasks by breaking them down into smaller parts.

Trying to be Perfect

Another problem that makes people procrastinate is perfectionism. People who want everything to be perfect often delay tasks because they worry their work won't be good enough, so they choose not to start at all. This creates a destructive cycle of worry and putting things off as the procrastinator gets more and more worried about not being able to be perfect, leading to even more delay.

Embracing Wabi-Sabi

Wabi-sabi is a Japanese philosophy that sees beauty and value in things that are not perfect, don't last forever and are not finished. It teaches us crucial lessons for overcoming the procrastination caused by wanting to be perfect.

Wabi-sabi shows us that there's something unique and exciting in things that are not perfect. Things like art, nature and important tasks come and go; over time, they will disappear or no longer be relevant. This way of thinking helps lessen the pressure to do a task perfectly, making you feel more relaxed and more likely to get it done. Wabi-sabi also teaches us to enjoy the journey and the process, not just the end result. Focusing on the experience of doing the work, where you're learning, growing and getting better, rather than only thinking about the final outcome, helps lower the fear of not being perfect and enables you to stop putting things off.

Another key lesson from Wabi-sabi is to let go of control. Often, people who want everything to be perfect feel they need to control everything they do, which is impossible because so many things are out of our control. You or a family member might get sick, or you might need to rely on someone else for part of the task but they are not available. Embracing Wabi-sabi means accepting that some things are beyond your control, and that's OK. This acceptance can help ease the worry that comes from wanting to be perfect and, as a result, procrastinating.

Decision Fatigue

When people have too many choices, they can get decision fatigue, sometimes called analysis paralysis. This happens when there are so many choices and decisions to make that they do not make any decisions. In today's fast-paced world, with so much choice and information, this can be a big problem. The tiredness from constantly making decisions can lead to putting things off, especially tasks that require lots of thinking and decision-making.

Making Hard Stuff Easy: Delegate, Automate, Eliminate

When making a big to-do list, my Delegate, Automate, Eliminate framework is an excellent way to reduce decision fatigue. This is a simpler version of the Eisenhower Matrix and can help you get important things done and focus less on small things, which people often put first when procrastinating.

Delegate

Identify Tasks for Delegation: review your task list and identify tasks that do not necessarily require your personal attention or expertise.

Assess Who Can Do It: determine if someone in your team, family or network has the skills and capacity to take on the task.

Provide Clear Instructions: when delegating, give clear, concise instructions to avoid confusion and ensure the task is completed effectively.

Follow-Up: establish a system for checking the task's progress without micromanaging.

Automate

Identify Recurring Tasks: identify regular tasks, like bill payments, report generation, social media posts or even household chores.

Choose the Right Tools: research and select automation tools or software that best fit the nature of the task. This could include setting up automatic payments, scheduling tools or employing smart home devices.

Set Up and Test: once you choose a tool, set up the automation and monitor it initially to ensure it's working as expected.

Regularly Review: periodically check the automated systems to ensure they are still functioning correctly and making the desired impact on your workload.

Eliminate

Assess Task Importance: critically evaluate each task and ask whether it truly adds value to your personal or professional goals.

Consider the Consequences: consider what would happen if the task were not done. If the impact is minimal or non-existent, it's a candidate for elimination.

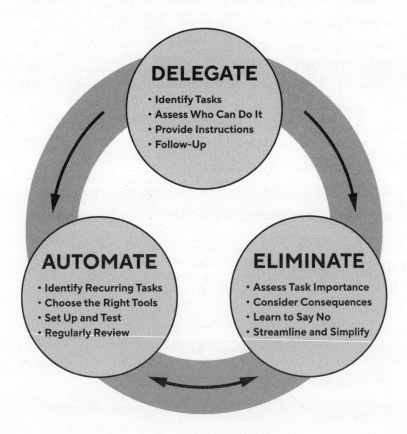

Learn to Say No: develop the habit of declining tasks or opportunities that do not align with your priorities or that add unnecessary complexity to your life.

Streamline and Simplify: look for ways to simplify tasks. Sometimes, tasks can't be eliminated entirely, but they can be simplified or reduced in scope.

#2 The Fear of Success

It's common to hear about the fear of failure, but not many people discuss the fear of success. If you've ever self-sabotaged, it's probably because of the fear of success. I'm going to explain three reasons why people might be afraid of being successful.

The Fear of Change

Becoming successful often means doing the hard stuff, like making sacrifices or changes in your life. These changes might include stopping certain habits or ending relationships that aren't good for you. People often mess things up for themselves because they're scared of turning into someone different. They worry about completely changing their lifestyle, relationships and identity. You might feel comfortable with who you are and what you're doing now, and the thought of how life could change if you start focusing on hard things can be frightening. But I'm here to tell you that your life won't get worse; it will get much better.

Making Hard Stuff Easy: Success Doesn't Change You; It Enhances Who You Are

When you tackle demanding tasks and succeed in what you're doing, it won't change who you are. It will just make you more of who you already are. If you're a kind and genuine person, success will make you even kinder and more genuine. But if you're an angry, unlikeable person, becoming successful might make you even more so.

The changes that usually happen when doing challenging things are about understanding who in your life is helping you and who is holding you back from reaching your goals. You'll probably have to make tough decisions, say goodbye to some 'friends' and change some of your routines. Still, each of these changes will only benefit you.

Imposter Syndrome

Imposter Syndrome is when you feel like you're not good enough and worry that others will find out you're not as capable or deserving as they think. Even when people do amazing things, they might still doubt their skills and think they haven't earned success.

If you've ever felt like an imposter, well done, you're just being human. It's a normal feeling and can be pretty helpful in the long run, as long as it doesn't take over your life. Adam Grant wrote a great book about Imposter Syndrome called *Think Again*. Here's something he said:

'The only people who never feel like imposters are narcissists. Being 100% sure of yourself at all times betrays arrogance and breeds complacency. Questioning yourself reflects humility and propels growth. Pangs of doubt are a normal, healthy human response to new challenges'

– Adam Grant

Imposters Don't Get Imposter Syndrome

A friend once told me, 'Imposters don't get imposter syndrome,' and it's really true. The opposite of someone with imposter syndrome is a person who's the real imposter as they think they're meant to be there and already know everything. This attitude is more harmful than good because it stops you from working on yourself to get better. One good thing about feeling like an imposter and doubting yourself is that if you don't let it stop you from tackling hard things, you'll work even harder.

Fear of the Peak

Another reason people are afraid of being successful is fear of the peak. This is the worry that once they reach their goals, they won't have anything left to aim for. They're scared they'll lose their drive or purpose.

In 1969, Buzz Aldrin was the second man to walk on the moon. After he came back to Earth, he was a hero in America. He travelled around the world, meeting influential leaders and being treated like a celebrity. But a few months later, Buzz started feeling down. He became sad, drank a lot and spent hours just lying in bed. Even his work as an engineer and scientist seemed pointless and unsatisfying.

This was because Buzz had reached his lifelong goal of walking on the moon but hadn't planned what he would do next. Buzz had hit the peak, but it was mostly in his mind because he still had many years left to do amazing things beyond landing on the moon.

There Will Always Be Mountains to Climb

What you need to remember about doing hard things and gaining success is that no matter what you achieve there will always be new challenges to face. To ensure you keep moving forward, it's important to set short- and long-term goals and have a lifelong purpose.

My short- or long-term goal might be to reach a certain weight or get a personal best time in a 5km run. But my lifelong purpose is to stay as healthy as possible, live a long life and see my children grow up and have their own lives. To do this, I need to keep fit and healthy, which means that my overall purpose continues even if I reach my goals. This purpose lets me set new short- and long-term goals to fulfil my lifelong aim.

#3 Lack of Motivation

Motivation can be hard to find, but we all want it. When you have it, everything seems easy and fun. It makes you feel like you're gliding through your tasks with excitement and energy.

But the problem with motivation is that it doesn't last. It's an emotion that comes and goes, so it's unreliable for always getting things done. Suppose you only work when you feel motivated? If that were the case, your work might be inconsistent and unproductive.

Discipline, on the other hand, is stronger and more reliable. It's not about how you feel. It's about thinking a certain way and practising self-control. Discipline is teaching yourself to follow the rules or stick to a particular way of doing things. It helps you get things done no matter how you're feeling. It's all about commitment, routine and pushing through even when you don't want to.

The big difference between motivation and discipline is how they relate to action and feeling. With motivation, you want to do something, and that feeling comes before you actually do it. Doing things when you're motivated is easy because you *already* want to. But with discipline you often have to do something even when you don't want to. The good feeling, like satisfaction or relief, comes *after* you finish the task.

MOTIVATION
The Feeling
Enabling you to do things when
you're motivated to do so

DISCIPLINE
The Thought Process
Enabling you to do things
regardless of how you feel

This shows why discipline is usually more helpful in the long run. Motivation can get you started, but discipline keeps you going, even when motivation fades. It's about building a way of thinking and habits that keep you moving forward and getting things done, even when you don't feel like doing anything.

So, while motivation is excellent to get you going, discipline is the more dependable way to achieve success in the long term. It means staying on track towards your goals, no matter how you feel.

Making Hard Stuff Easy: Challenge Yourself

Building discipline means you must trust yourself for a while until you begin seeing the benefits of your new thinking. Consider what you're finding hard to feel motivated about, then set yourself a challenge to do it daily for thirty days. This could be taking a cold shower each morning, stretching, committing to fifty push-ups or something as simple as going to bed earlier.

When you stick to a task for a whole month, it helps you form a habit. It's not just about doing the task but also about building the routine. At first, it might feel difficult or strange, but it gets easier as the days go by. You start getting used to the new activity, which quickly becomes a regular part of your day.

This thirty-day challenge is an excellent way to prove that you can stick to something and progress. It's also a chance to see the changes and benefits that come from your effort. You might feel healthier, have more energy or be proud that you kept your promise to yourself.

The idea isn't to do something impossible. The goal is to choose something manageable that still challenges you. It's about taking small, consistent steps that add to significant changes. By the end of the thirty days, you'll not only have achieved something but also developed a stronger sense of discipline that you can apply to other areas of your life.

#4 Lack of Accountability

When doing demanding tasks, we often find it easy to let ourselves off the hook, but it's harder to let others down. We tend to choose the easier option when it's just us, but we care about how others see us. To keep up our image and avoid embarrassment, we're more likely to do difficult things if we promise others we will. Being accountable to others helps in three ways:

Social Accountability

We're naturally social and how we're perceived by others can really push us to do things. Studies in social psychology have shown that people are more likely to follow through on commitments when they have to report their progress to someone else.

Making Hard Stuff Easy: 'Paying' Attention

One way of significantly improving your chances of success by doing hard stuff is by putting some skin in the game and paying for someone to hold you accountable. When you pay someone, you pay more attention, as this exchange signals to yourself that you care about it more.

Fear of Social Judgement

The fear of negative judgement or disappointing others can be a stronger push than just trying to hold yourself accountable.

People often prioritize external commitments due to concerns about how failing to meet them might affect how others perceive them.

Making Hard Stuff Easy: Find a Battle Buddy

Whenever we work with others in a group-based setting, we first establish what are known as battle buddies. Battle buddies are a small group of like-minded people focusing on achieving a similar outcome-based goal. When you surround yourself with people and promise to be there for them, it's a lot easier to accomplish hard stuff.

The Hawthorne Effect

The Hawthorne effect is named after research done in the 1920s and 1930s at the Hawthorne Works of the Western Electric Company. The researchers examined how different working conditions affected how much work was done by the employees. What they found was a surprise. Any change they made, good or bad, seemed to make the workers do more for a short time. The researchers figured out that it wasn't the changes to the work area that made the difference. It was because the workers knew they were being watched. Knowing this changed how they acted. This behaviour change might have been because they wanted to look good, were scared of being criticized or naturally reacted to getting attention.

Making Hard Stuff Easy: Choosing a Public Commitment

I've used the Hawthorne effect for years to achieve some great things. The hardest part has been to tell the public what I will do and when. It's incredible how much your actions change and how you push to get tough things done when you know people are watching.

#5 No Clear Direction or Path

When you start challenging tasks without clear goals or a set direction, they can seem scarier than they really are. This is because not having a clear end goal makes it hard to see how you're doing, making you feel overwhelmed or lost.

Having clear goals is like having a map. It guides you, gives you a reason to keep going and helps break the task into smaller, more manageable chunks. This way, you can handle each part one by one.

Knowing exactly what you need to do gives you focus. It helps you use your time and energy better.

Here are three things that can go wrong when you're not sure where you're going:

Doubt and half-hearted efforts: if you're unsure you're on the right path, you might not give it your all. This is because you fear wasting your effort if you need to change direction. This can become a self-fulfilling prophecy in that you don't try hard enough and then fail, making you think not trying was the right choice.

*'Accountability is the glue that ties
the commitment to the result'*

– Bob Proctor

The 'what if' scenario: not being sure often leads to many 'what if' thoughts. You keep questioning your choices, which can stop you from doing anything. This is another self-fulfilling prophecy where doubting your decisions prevents you from acting. Then you don't get the result, proving your doubts right.

The risk of regret: being scared that you'll regret the effort you put into the wrong path can freeze you in your tracks. It's your brain trying to avoid future disappointment. I often see people who do something and get an OK result but then say, 'Imagine if I'd really tried.' This way of thinking is flawed. They're so scared of giving their all and maybe not winning or succeeding that they never give 100 per cent to anything.

Making Hard Stuff Easy: Planning Your Path

Step One - Clarity: first, be clear about what you want to achieve. Use SMART goals: Specific, Measurable, Achievable, Relevant and Time-Bound. Instead of just saying you want to lose weight, set a goal like this: 'I aim to lose 10lbs in the next twelve weeks by walking 10,000 steps a day, watching what I eat and going to the gym four times a week.'

Step Two - Timeline/Deadline: give yourself enough time to reach your goal and set a deadline. This makes it more likely you'll get there. Remember Parkinson's Law: *a task will take as long as the time you give it*. But be realistic with your timeline.

Step Three - Commitments/Non-Negotiables: think about who you'll make a promise to when it comes to reaching your goal. Will you tell everyone or just a close friend?

Step Four - Measurement/Management: As Peter Drucker said, 'What gets measured, gets managed.' Your SMART goals highlight three things to track and manage: your steps, eating and gym visits. Keeping track helps you adjust if you hit a plateau, like increasing steps, eating less or going to the gym more.

Step Five - Accountability/Support: write down how you'll keep yourself on track and who you can rely on for support when things get tough.

Step Six - Flexibility/Refocus: be clear on your goals, but flexible in your approach. Life can sometimes disrupt our plans, so be ready to adjust your methods. There's often more than one way to reach a goal.

Step Seven - Routines/Rewards: plan your weekly routines and put them in your calendar to build habits. Also, decide on a reward for achieving your goal. Many people forget to celebrate their victories. When you succeed, treat yourself to something special. This positive reinforcement makes setting and achieving future goals easier.

Building Resilience Through Challenges

A significant part of tackling challenging tasks is about developing resilience. Resilience is how well you can recover from difficult times. Every time we face and get through challenging situations, we get better at dealing with tough times. Life often tests how resilient we are. Instead of just waiting for life to make us stronger, we can work on building our resilience ourselves. To do this well, it's essential to know about the four main types of resilience we face in life and how to get better at each one.

Emotional Resilience

Emotional resilience is getting over and adjusting to emotional problems, setbacks or upsetting events. It means handling your feelings well, keeping your emotions steady and recovering quickly from emotional upset.

How to Build Your Emotional Resilience: Calm Amid Chaos

Building your emotional resilience can be significantly enhanced by learning to keep calm in chaotic situations. When everything around you seems overwhelming, staying calm helps you think clearly and respond better. You can practise this by taking deep breaths, stepping back from the situation to gain perspective or engaging in activities that relax you, like meditation or a short walk. This calm approach allows you to manage your emotions effectively, preventing panic and rash decisions. Over time, this habit builds your emotional resilience. It equips you to handle life's challenges with a composed and clear mind.

Mental Resilience

Mental resilience is about having a strong mind that lets you deal with stress, tough times and high-pressure situations. It includes being mentally tough, staying focused and keeping your thoughts clear even when things are hard.

Physical Resilience

Physical resilience is about how well your body can handle physical challenges, get better from injuries or sickness, and stay healthy and strong even under stress.

How to Build Your Mental and Physical Resilience: Get Out of Your Comfort Zone

Building your mental and physical resilience can be significantly enhanced by challenging yourself to do something entirely outside your comfort zone at least once a year. Whether running a marathon, learning a new skill or even travelling solo to a foreign country, this challenge pushes your boundaries and tests your limits. These experiences strengthen your mental toughness as you navigate the unfamiliar or challenging and improve your physical resilience, as many out-of-comfort-zone activities involve a physical component, too. Challenging yourself like this once a year will give you something to add to the 'Cookie Jar', which we will discuss later.

Professional Resilience

Professional resilience is about adjusting to changes and challenging situations at work, like problems in your career, new roles and stress in the workplace. It means keeping up with your work, handling work relationships well and sticking to your career aims even when things get complicated.

How to build your Professional Resilience: Practise Stress Resilience in the Workplace

To build your professional resilience, it's essential to develop the skills to handle challenging situations directly in your work environment rather than relying solely on coping methods outside of work. By confronting these challenges head-on during your workday, you strengthen your ability to respond effectively under pressure. This might include learning to communicate more effectively, prioritizing tasks or seeking feedback to improve.

Making Hard Stuff Easy: The 'Cookie Jar' Approach

David Goggins, a renowned ultramarathon runner, ultra-distance cyclist, triathlete and retired Navy SEAL, introduced the concept of the cookie jar as a mental strategy for being mentally stronger, more resilient and believing more in your abilities.

What Is It?

Goggins's cookie jar is a symbolic place where he stores his past accomplishments and the challenges he's overcome. These can range from life's major triumphs to everyday struggles.

How It Works

Whenever Goggins faces a new challenge or finds himself in a situation where he needs an extra push, he mentally reaches into this cookie jar and reminds himself of his past successes and the difficulties he has already conquered. This serves as a reminder of his strength, resilience and ability to overcome hardships.

Each challenge you overcome can be placed in the cookie jar

and shows you are capable, tough and resilient. It's a personal history of triumphs you can draw upon in times of need.

The point of the cookie jar method is to change how you think, from doubting yourself to believing in yourself. When you're up against something new and challenging, instead of worrying about whether you can do it, you think about all the times you've succeeded. This change in how you see things is critical to facing challenging tasks.

It's also about getting past mental blocks. By remembering the tough times you've already beaten, you can fight the doubts and negative thoughts that might stop you when facing something challenging.

How to Use the 'Cookie Jar' Approach

Make your own cookie jar: anyone can create their own cookie jar. It's about remembering all the good things you've done and hard times you've got through.

Everyday challenges: this idea isn't just for extreme sportspeople or soldiers. It can help with simple work problems, personal goals or fitness targets.

Long-term benefits: regularly using this strategy can change how you see yourself and how you handle stress and difficult times.

The cookie jar is a solid mental tool for building a collection of your successes. It's about focusing on your strength and resilience based on your own experiences of overcoming challenges. Its goal is to make you more resilient, confident and ready to take on demanding tasks with a can-do attitude.

Notes

Epilogue

Every Transformation Starts From the Neck Up

Seven years before writing this book, I went through one of the most challenging times in my life.

The year was 2016 and it had kicked off brilliantly. I was ticking off all my goals, achieving everything I had set out to do. It looked like I was on top of the world. But, as the year ended, despite all these successes, I felt utterly shattered and miserable. I had thought I was wrapping up the final chapter in my own story of understanding myself, becoming successful, managing my emotions and staying strong when times were hard. But I was just starting out.

This challenging time in my life was a huge wake-up call. It made me stop and think about many things I had always believed were true. I had to step back and start over, rethinking and rebuilding each part of my thinking. It was like putting together a jigsaw puzzle, with each piece a new idea or way of looking at things.

During this period, I learned so much about myself. I realized that success isn't just about ticking goals off a list; it's about feeling good inside, too. I also learned that it's OK to feel down sometimes and that dealing with these feelings is a big part of success.

I started to see that life is full of ups and downs, and that that's normal. The important thing is how we handle these moments. This time of change helped me understand that being strong isn't just about pushing through tough times; it's also about being able to change and adapt when needed.

I've put all these lessons and more into this book. It's a collection of everything I've learned from that hard time. I hope that by sharing my stories and what I've learned, I can help you with your challenges. Maybe this book can be a friend to you in tough times, offering ideas and ways of thinking to make your journey easier.

A simple yet powerful truth is that transformation starts from the neck up. The stories and lessons I've shared in this book all hinge on the idea that our thoughts, mental attitudes and perceptions hold the key to unlocking a life that's not just bearable but beautiful in every aspect. The possibility for change resides in our mental processes.

We've covered a lot of ground. We've talked about finding happiness, controlling our thoughts, loving ourselves and much more. Each chapter has been like a piece of a puzzle. When we put these pieces together, they show us how we can have a better life by changing how we think.

As we start this last chapter, remember that the changes we're looking for – feeling better, growing and being happy – all begin in our minds. It's in our thoughts and beliefs that we start making changes. And it's from these changes that our lives begin to get better.

Principle 1: Happiness is an Inside Job
Developing Unconditional Happiness

In our world, there's an exceptional type of happiness. It's the sort that wells up deep inside you, not dependent on external events or circumstances. This is what we call unconditional happiness. Unconditional happiness means finding joy regardless of what life may throw your way. It isn't tied to the material possessions you own, the people you are surrounded by or even the situations you encounter. It's about maintaining a sense of inner contentment, even when things outside aren't aligning with your idea of perfect.

Altering your mindset is the key to tapping into this sort of happiness. Imagine it as flipping a switch in your brain. Instead of holding out for everything to align perfectly before allowing yourself to feel happy, you consciously embrace happiness in the present moment just as things stand. This approach involves being happy irrespective of the external environment and ongoing events.

Remember, happiness isn't a treasure to be hunted down in the external world; it's a state of being that we can cultivate and nurture within ourselves. Embracing this understanding is genuinely the initial step in transforming our lives. It involves learning to be happy simply because we choose to be independent of our external circumstances.

Principle 2: Make Peace With Your Past
Getting Control of Rumination

One of the most significant changes that can positively impact your life is when you concentrate on creating and enhancing your mental tools to combat overthinking. When we ruminate, we're caught in a loop, endlessly replaying the same worries and problems. Our minds get stuck in replay mode, constantly bringing up negative thoughts. This habit can wreak havoc in our lives, leading our daily stress and anxiety levels to skyrocket.

The crucial step to break free from this rumination cycle is to transform these repetitive thoughts into something constructive rather than obstructive. Instead of repeatedly mulling over the same concerns, we can focus on finding solutions or reminding ourselves of the positive aspects of our lives. It's about redirecting your mind from a spinning wheel of worries to a more serene and positive space.

Altering our thought patterns is challenging but vital for internal well-being. Gaining control over our thoughts, preventing them from spiralling into endless loops, brings a sense of calm and peace. Our thoughts significantly influence our emotions, and by steering our mindset from negative to positive, we can uplift our mood and overall happiness. Taking control of our thoughts is an important stride towards achieving a happier, more tranquil life.

By consciously focusing on positive outcomes and solutions rather than dwelling on problems, we empower ourselves to live more fulfilling lives. This approach doesn't just reduce stress and anxiety; it opens up new possibilities for joy and contentment. When we learn to guide our thoughts in a constructive direction, we improve our mental health and our overall quality of life. So embracing this shift in thinking is not just about avoiding negative thoughts; it's about paving the way for a happier, more balanced existence.

Principle 3: Love Yourself
The Importance of Self-Love

One of the harshest critics we encounter in life is often ourselves. For many, it's a relentless cycle of finding faults and blaming oneself. The journey to self-love starts when you shift from thinking negatively about yourself to adopting a kinder and more positive mindset.

Loving yourself affects everything – how you feel, how you act and how you treat other people. When you think good things about yourself, you start to take better care of yourself and feel more confident. Being kind to ourselves in our thoughts is the first step to a happier and more loving life.

Remember that loving yourself starts in the mind, and when you become kind and your best supporter, you start to feel better about who you are. This is not to say you ignore your mistakes, but you learn to be gentle and understanding with yourself, just like you would be with a good friend.

When you love yourself, it's easier to find joy in small things and face challenges with resilience. This self-compassion leads to better stress management and healthier relationships, as you are more empathetic and understanding towards others. Embracing self-love is not just about feeling good; it's about creating a positive cycle where your improved self-view positively impacts all areas of your life. In essence, self-love is critical to unlocking a more contented, more loving existence.

Principle 4: No One Cares
Overcoming the Spotlight Effect

Most people believe they're constantly under scrutiny, with everyone around them watching and judging their every move. There's this persistent feeling that we're always in the spotlight, with every action noticed. However, the truth is quite different. In reality, most people are too wrapped up in their own lives to pay close attention to what we're doing.

When you finally grasp and, more importantly, move beyond this notion, it's incredible to discover the sense of freedom that comes from realizing you're not always the centre of attention. This understanding liberates us from the constant worry about others' opinions, lifting the burden we often carry on our shoulders.

This shift in perspective can lead to a more carefree and enjoyable existence. We become less concerned with making mistakes or being judged, which encourages us to try new things and express ourselves more openly. This newfound freedom can improve our relationships as we interact more genuinely and less guardedly. Understanding and overcoming the spotlight effect is a crucial step towards a more relaxed, confident and enjoyable life.

Principle 5: Don't Allow Feelings to Affect Your Future
Weathering the Storm of Emotions

Throughout our lives, there are times when our emotions can feel overwhelming, like a tumultuous storm raging inside us. Learning to navigate and manage these intense feelings is crucial. It's about developing the ability to remain steadfast and resilient, even when emotional turmoil seems to be at its peak.

This process is fundamentally about building emotional resilience, which is really just mental strength. It is the capacity to recover quickly from difficulties; it's about not allowing challenging emotions to keep us down for long. Cultivating this strength begins with our thoughts. It involves understanding the reasons behind our feelings and adopting thought patterns that help us cope.

Managing our emotions doesn't mean we don't experience them deeply. Instead, it's about not allowing our feelings to take the driver's seat. Feeling sadness, anger or fear is normal, but these emotions don't have to dominate us. By gaining insight into our thoughts, we learn to steer them constructively, allowing us to handle our emotions more adeptly. This skill helps us maintain a sense of calm and control, even in challenging situations.

When we practise this kind of emotional management, we improve our ability to deal with the present and safeguard our future. By not letting temporary emotions dictate our long-term decisions, we can make choices more aligned with our overall goals and well-being. This ability to weather emotional storms equips us to face life's ups and downs with a steadier heart and mind, ensuring that our future is not swayed by transient feelings.

Principle 6: Be Present
Mastering Mindfulness

Mindfulness is the practice of focusing intently on what's happening in our surroundings and within ourselves while deliberately avoiding getting swept up in reflections on the past or concerns about the future.

To excel in mindfulness, it's necessary to cultivate a specific type of mental discipline. We must train our minds to remain anchored in the present moment, resisting the tendency to drift away into daydreams or worries. As with many of the concepts discussed in this book, achieving mindfulness is a challenging but crucial skill to develop. As we practise and improve our mindfulness, we observe details and nuances in our everyday experiences that might previously have eluded us.

Being fully present allows us to engage with life more intensely. It's akin to viewing the world in more vivid colours. Our senses are heightened – we hear more clearly, see more vividly and feel more deeply, enriching and adding layers of complexity to our lives. By anchoring ourselves in the now, we enhance our experiences and strengthen our connection to the world around us.

This enhanced awareness can lead to a deeper appreciation of life's simple joys, like the sun's warmth on our skin or the sound of laughter. It encourages a sense of gratitude and can improve our overall well-being. Practising mindfulness can reduce stress, increase our enjoyment of life and foster a sense of peace and contentment. In short, mastering mindfulness is not just about improving our focus; it's about enriching our entire life experience.

Principle 7: Hard Stuff, Easy Life; Easy Stuff, Hard Life
Doing the Hard Stuff for an Easy Life

Improving our ability to manage difficult situations can significantly ease our life journey. It's about cultivating the mental fortitude needed to approach life's challenges positively and enthusiastically.

The initial step is to mentally commit to facing these challenges head-on. It's about making a firm decision that we won't back down regardless of the difficulties. Adopting this mindset of resilience is crucial in empowering us to overcome challenging circumstances.

Every time we confront a difficult task and succeed, we strengthen. It's akin to exercising a muscle – the more we use it, the more robust it becomes. By bravely facing adversity instead of avoiding it, we surmount the immediate challenge and accumulate valuable life lessons. These experiences enrich our perspective and serve as reference points for future challenges, enhancing our ability to handle whatever life may throw our way.

This process of confronting and overcoming obstacles is transformative. It not only builds our resilience but also boosts our confidence. We start to trust our ability to navigate challenging times, knowing that we've done it before and can do it again. This confidence, in turn, makes future challenges seem less daunting. By consistently facing and overcoming these challenges, we equip ourselves with a tool kit of skills and experiences that make us more adept at handling life's complexities. In essence, learning to deal with difficult things not only prepares us for future hurdles but also contributes to a more fulfilling and resilient life.

Final Thoughts

It all starts and ends in our heads. When we change how we think, we change how we live. Learning to be happy no matter what, controlling our thoughts, loving ourselves and staying in the present moment are all changes that begin in our minds. It's like planting a seed; as it grows, it changes how you see and do things.

Our mental changes are the first steps to seeing fundamental, noticeable changes in our lives. When we think differently, we start to act differently. These actions then lead to better experiences and a better life. Significant changes in our lives begin with minor changes in our thoughts.

As we come to the end of the book, I want to encourage you to keep going on your journey of changing your mind for the better. Remember, this isn't something that happens overnight. It's an ongoing process. Just as plants need regular care to grow, our minds need ongoing attention and work to keep growing well.

Think of each day as a new chance to practise your learning. Whether it's being more present, handling challenging emotions or thinking positively about yourself, every small step you take is essential. And when things don't go as planned, remember that's OK too. Growing and changing means learning from mistakes and not giving up.

Mental growth has ups and downs, but each step forward moves you towards a happier, more fulfilling life. Keep your spirits up, keep learning and keep growing. Your mind is a powerful tool; with care and effort, it can lead you to beautiful places.

As you close the pages of *Hard Stuff, Easy Life*, let's remember a fundamental lesson we've learned together: when we tackle the tough stuff in our minds, life gets easier. Just as the title of this book says, it's the hard work we do inside our heads that paves the way for a smoother, happier path in life.

You should feel proud of yourself for setting off on this journey. You've already taken significant steps by reading this book and making these changes. And the exciting part? This is just the beginning. With the tools and ideas we've explored, you're ready to face life with a stronger, more positive mindset.

Endless possibilities are waiting for you. With a mind prepared to think positively, handle emotions well and stay present, you can achieve so much more than you might think. Remember, the power to improve your life lies within you. Carry this hope and empowerment with you as you enter the future. Keep believing in yourself, growing and looking forward to all the fantastic things you can do.

Acknowledgements

To my wife Anna,

Words alone cannot fully capture the depth of my gratitude for your abiding love and support by my side over the past twenty-five years. This past year especially, as I poured my whole heart and soul into writing, your faith in me kept me persevering.

I simply could not have walked this winding writing road without your support. You have been my muse, editor, sounding board, sanctuary and, most of all, my loving companion through laughter and tears on this crazy journey through life.

My precious daughter, Elyza,

Words alone cannot express the joy and pride that fills my heart whenever I call you 'my daughter'. You have been one of my most significant sources of inspiration and purpose since I first held you in my arms.

Life's sweetest blessing is watching you grow into a thoughtful, kind-hearted and determined young woman. Your passion for learning, creativity and improving the world is contagious. Through this book, I hope to make you proud and pass on life lessons that have guided me along the way. But the truth is, you already make me swell with pride each and every day. I dedicate this book to you, my darling daughter and my daily inspiration.

Thank you for filling my heart with joy and giving me the courage to face new challenges.

My dearest son, Archer,

Before you were born, I wondered how I could love another child as much as I loved your sister. But holding you in my arms for the first time showed me that a parent's love is not divided but multiplied.

Through this book, I hope to impart the life lessons and timeless wisdom that have guided me along the often rocky road of life. I want to equip you with the resilience, self-knowledge and strength of character to thrive amid adversity. When the path gets complicated, as it surely will, I will be there with an outstretched hand, ready to lift you up or walk beside you.

You, my beautiful boy, give me joy and purpose every day. Thank you for your forgiving heart when I fall short, as I surely will. And for giving me the priceless gift of being your dad. I am so very proud of you.

To Karolina,

I am deeply grateful for your pivotal role in bringing this book to fruition. Your enthusiasm and dedication to this project have been invaluable from the start.

Your support and belief in my work have been a tremendous source of motivation, empowering me to push creative boundaries and strive for excellence.

This book simply would not exist without you. Your faith in its potential inspired me during moments of doubt and uncertainty, and your contributions to this book and my growth as a writer will forever be appreciated.

Notes